30 5 1970   ~~£ 3.95~~
2.⁰⁰

FAMOUS REGIMENTS

The Rhodesian African Rifles

FAMOUS REGIMENTS

Edited by
Lt.-General Sir Brian Horrocks

The Rhodesian
African Rifles

by Christopher Owen

Leo Cooper Ltd., London

Made in Great Britain at the Pitman Press, Bath

". . . To dare boldly,
In a fair cause, and for their country's safety:
To run upon the cannon's mouth undaunted;
To obey their leaders, and shun mutinies;
To bear with patience the winter's cold
And summer's scorching heat, and not to faint
When plenty of provision fails, with hunger,
Are the essential parts that make up a soldier."

PHILLIP MASSINGER

INTRODUCTION TO THE SERIES
by Lt.-General Sir Brian Horrocks

THE AUTHOR, Christopher Owen, has managed with great skill to avoid politics of any sort, and in this brief introduction I will try to follow suit. But I cannot refrain from saying that I hope this excellent short history will be widely publicised in the U.K., because it is quite time that we emerged, if only for a short period, from the political morass in which we are now floundering and remembered the splendid response of this small colony of Rhodesia during the last war—particularly in the early stages when, almost alone, Britain was fighting with its back to the wall.

In 1939 throughout the whole colony approximately 10,000 white Rhodesians were available and fit for active service; of these 6,500 eventually served outside Rhodesia. So much for the white contribution.

In June 1940 a regiment, subsequently called the Rhodesian African Rifles, was formed under Major Wane. Fortunately it came of distinguished parentage, namely the Rhodesian Native Regiment, which during the First World War had fought with distinction against the most elusive and skilful General von Lettow-Vorbeck in German East Africa. Although this unit had long since been disbanded it had provided an askari unit in the British South Africa Police and it was from this source that the first African N.C.O.s were obtained. So the tradition of military service in aid of the British Empire already existed among the older members of the colony. This was just as well, because the newly formed R.A.R. with its British officers and British African N.C.O.s and men was to suffer every kind of frustration in its early years. The old Army saying 'order, counter-order, disorder certainly applied in this case and had there not been complete confidence and affection between officer and askari, the African Rifles could have died from that most pernicious disease—boredom.

It is to their eternal credit that they survived and distinguished themselves in one of the least known but most difficult campaigns fought during the last war, namely in the Arakan, with its sharp razor-like mountain ridges covered with seemingly impenetrable jungle. And it was in this type of warfare that the Japanese were such dangerous opponents.

What makes this book so readable are the human stories which the author has unearthed from the officers and men themselves. Let me give you just one example:

'Old hands still recall the Battalion Parade which turned into a riot when a hare rather foolishly chose to loiter on the edge of the parade ground. With one accord and with excited shrill whoops the men broke ranks and gave chase, ignoring their cursing and shouting officers until the hare was finally caught.'

No Askari has ever been able to resist a hunt.

The spirit of the regiment can best be summed up in the words of their African Regimental Sergeant-Major Stephen Machado, written after the war when they had returned to Rhodesia:

'And today we all smile together. For have we not fought and risked our lives side by side to keep our land safe from the horrible things we have seen.'

Subsequently the Regiment served in the Canal Zone and then for two years against the Communist guerillas in Malaya. Today it is once more engaged in jungle warfare but this time nearer home, in the Zambesi valley along their own northern border. Let us hope that Stephen Machado's words hold good.

Acknowledgements

A large debt of gratitude is owed Lieutenant-Colonel
G. E. L. (Kim) Rule, O.B.E., both by myself and by the
Regiment. During his years as Commanding Officer of
the Rhodesian African Rifles he had the foresight to collect,
and collate, as much as he could of its history. He has
freely made available the result of his labours, and I am
very grateful.

My thanks are also accorded the following former
members of the Regiment for their suggestions, corrections,
and (above all) reminiscences: Lieutenant-Colonel G. E.
Wells, C.B.E., E.D.; Major C. S. Davies; Major M. E.
Mills; and Major T. J. B. Baxter.

I am deeply obliged to Mr. Burke of the National
Archives for his unfailingly courteous help and advice,
and to the Rt. Hon. Sir Robert Tredgold, K.C.M.G.,
Q.C., who provided me with much of the material relating
to the political issues described in Chapter One.

Finally, my grateful thanks to Lieutenant-Colonel W. H.
Godwin, O.B.E., under whom I served when he commanded the Regiment, and whose enthusiasm first inspired
this short work.

January, 1970   CHRISTOPHER OWEN

Maps

Chapter

I

The Birth of the Regiment

THE following entry appears in the Rhodesian Defence Headquarters War Diary, datelined June 17, 1940:

"Rhodesian African Rifles:
Major F. J. Wane appointed Officer Commanding the Rhodesian African Rifles, for which recruiting and training of instructors has been proceeding for some time. European N.C.O.'s to be recruited mainly from the British South Africa Police and the Native Department, appointed as sergeants, and posted to commissioned rank at a later date on ability. Native rates of pay vary from one shilling a day as privates, to two shillings a day as Regimental Sergeant-Major, plus rations."

This brief statement, bearing the full weight of military authority, seemed to give—as no previous sanction had done—official recognition to the birth of the Rhodesian African Rifles. It marked also the beginning-of-the-end of a long, and often bitter, public controversy which had preceded the formation of the Regiment.

Many months before the start of World War II far-sighted men in Rhodesian political and military circles had begun a quiet campaign. They wanted nothing less than to see the establishment of an armed unit of regular African soldiers. The danger was obvious. At that time the Colony was populated by only 75,000 Europeans compared to 3,000,000 Africans. Outnumbered thirty-six to one, was it sensible to arm and (even more importantly) train a unit that could provide a hard core of disciplined leadership for insurrection?

The idea was radical, of course, but it was not without precedent, for the Rhodesian Native Regiment had been raised during World War I, and had fought with distinction against von Lettow-Vorbeck in German East Africa. Although disbanded immediately after the war, the Regiment had provided the nucleus for an askari unit in the British South Africa Police, and it was from this small group that the Rhodesian African Rifles was later to obtain its first African non-commissioned officers.

As is the unfortunate case with most armies in peace time, however, the loyal service of the Rhodesian Native Regiment during the Great War had been conveniently forgotten by 1939. Instead many Europeans in the Colony, as soon as they realised the import of what was being proposed, rose in protest. The newspapers were filled with letters asserting that the inevitable result of arming and training a large body of Africans would be the extinction of the white man in Rhodesia. They reminded the nation (in lucid and horrifying detail) of the Matabele and Mashona rebellions which had ravaged the country a little more than forty years ago. These few but very vocal dissidents aroused considerable support. Undaunted by the opposition, but nevertheless treading carefully, the project's champions continued to advance their ideas. Their first suggestion (raised in the Legislative Assembly) proposed that an African cyclist battalion should be formed, emphasizing, as its prime attraction, the special mobility of such a unit under local conditions. The reaction to this suggestion was so violently unfavourable that it was hurriedly withdrawn and forgotten. It was then suggested that a non-combatant battalion be raised, with the hope that later, when the public had accepted the idea, it could be converted into an armed unit. This, too, was received without enthusiasm, the principal objection being that it was not thought likely that many Europeans would be attracted to a non-combatant unit with the prospect of serious fighting looming in the near future.

Then, on September 3, 1939, war was declared and it soon became obvious that Rhodesia was over-straining herself in her ambitious contribution to the general war effort. In 1939 there were approximately 10,000 white Rhodesians available for active service. Of these, some 6,500 eventually served outside the Colony. This created a series of increasingly awkward problems, not the least of which was that, with nearly seventy per cent of Rhodesia's available white military manpower serving outside her borders, the country's internal security had become somewhat compromised. Seen in this light, objections to the proposed African battalion suddenly melted away, and most of those who had opposed the formation of the battalion now became its firm supporters. With the political doubts resolved, the military authorities were free to act, and in May 1940 initiated the formation of the unit.

Naturally enough, the decision did not please everyone, and a number of people continued to agitate against it, especially certain members of the farming community. The United Kingdom, in assessing the Commonwealth war effort, had laid particular stress on the importance of Rhodesia maintaining full agricultural production. As labourers, the Africans played a vital part in maintaining this production and many of the leading members of the colony's agricultural industry made gloomy public speeches warning that Rhodesia would suffer serious agricultural loss. Typical of these is a speech made by an executive of the then Rhodesian Agricultural Union on June 18, 1940: "When natives are recruited for the native regiment there will be no spare labour left in the reserves to form labour gangs to assist farms." When commenting on this speech, the Editor of the *Rhodesia Herald* pointed out that there were 282,000 male adult Africans in the Colony, and "when it is realised that two native regiments would represent less than one per cent" of this total, it made the argument frivolous. Finally, the Prime Minister (Sir Godfrey Huggins) broadcasting to the nation on June 25, stated in his typical outspoken way, "It is not expected that the native units will deplete primary production by more than one per cent at the most, but if they do it cannot be helped;" and thus deflated the last of the opposition.

Even when South Africa made it known that she was alarmed by the prospect of armed Africans on her northern border, the Rhodesian Government, having made up its mind, would not be dissuaded. In fact, within a few short months of its inception, an extraordinary surge of feeling for the new regiment began to grip the general public. White Rhodesians took the Battalion to their hearts, and any parade always attracted an enthusiastic audience. It was soon apparent that the regiment was regarded with widespread pride and affection.

In the beginning of 1940, Major F. J. Wane, who had served with distinction during the First World War with the Rhodesian Native Regiment, was living in retirement from the Native Department on his farm in the Umvukwes. His retirement plans were interrupted in early May, however, when Defence Headquarters notified him that an African battalion was being formed and that he was offered command. Wane accepted readily, but apart from this bare decision to form the Battalion very little else in the way of preparation seems to have been done. Major Wane had to start from scratch. For an office he was given a table in an already occupied room at Defence Headquarters, and it was left to his own initiative to scrounge pens, paper and other normal office equipment. As for barracks in which to house the Regiment—there were none. On June 27, the Salisbury Town Council agreed therefore to rent to the Government—without charge for the duration of the war—the Municipal Farm which stood on the Borrowdale Road some three miles north-east of

the town. Here the Regiment was to establish its camp.
There were no buildings on the site. As the Secretary
for Defence was to report, rather laconically, to the Legislative Assembly: "The initial training of the Regiment was
impeded by the fact that their barracks of pole and dagga
huts had to be built by themselves." These were insignifi-
cant beginnings—a table in Defence Headquarters, a few
acres of Municipal farmland—but it was perhaps their
very inconsequence that fostered a vigorous *esprit de corps*
which was soon to make itself felt throughout the new
Battalion.

Meanwhile, at about the same time as Wane had received
his summons, twenty members of the Police Force had
been posted to the Regiment. After an intensive six-weeks
refresher course in drill and weapon handling they were
pronounced ready to begin instructing the African recruits,
numbers of whom had already started to enlist. Then a
further twenty young men were recruited (nineteen from
the Native Department, and one from the Southern
Rhodesia Staff Corps) and sent to the Military Training
Camp at Bulawayo. The camp was then commanded by
Captain G. E. Wells who later became the Battalion second-
in-command under Colonel Wane. After a ten-week course
of training, they too were dispatched to Borrowdale
Camp along with one man from the Army Ordnance
Branch, posted to deal with administrative matters. By
July 19, 1940, when Government Notice 374/1940 was
published, charging the Regiment with: "The defence of the
Colony, the maintenance of order, and such other duties
as the Minister may define," it had become, very obviously,
a going concern.

From the start an intensive drive had been made for
African recruits. Members of the Native Department made
spirited addresses to large audiences of urban Africans
in the local townships, and Native Commissioners in the
rural areas were asked to publicise the call to arms. The

following advertisement was inserted in all the Colony's newspapers, printed in various African dialects as well as in English:

> 'Those who wish to serve their King should apply to the nearest Native Commissioner's office, where particulars of service can be obtained, and tickets for the journey to Salisbury issued to those who are passed medically fit. Rates of pay are as under:

Regimental Sergeant-Major	...	...	2/- per diem
Enlisted Native Schoolmaster	...	...	2/- „ „
Company Sergeant-Major	...	...	1/8 „ „
Enlisted Native Clerk	...	...	1/8 „ „
Sergeant ...	...	...	...	... 1/4 „ „
Corporal ...	...	...	...	... 1/2 „ „
Lance-Corporal ...	...	...	... 1/1 „ „
Private ...	...	...	...	... 1/- „ „

> Conditions of service also include free clothing, rations and quarters. Commanding this Regiment is Colonel Wane (Msoro-we-gomo) who is known to most Africans in Rhodesia.'

The use of Wane's African name (roughly, "the top of the mountain"), and the tone of the final paragraph recall the time when there were relatively few Europeans in Rhodesia, and those employed by the Native Department were usually well known to the majority of Africans throughout the Colony. Wane was unquestionably popular and it was the magic of "Msoro-we-gomo" which achieved the enthusiastic initial rush of recruits. One result of the recruiting programme, however, puzzled the authorities: the majority of recruits came from the Mashona tribes and very few from the Matabele—cousins of the Zulu and traditionally the warrior clan of Rhodesia. It had been expected that the Matabele would be among the first to enlist. Investigation soon revealed that trouble-makers had been spreading a rumour—totally untrue—that the officers and non-commissioned officers of the Battalion could not speak Sindebele. The agitators pointed out that this would result in Matabele soldiers being ignored, and probably neglected in preferment. The rumour, allied to the natural disinclination of the Matabele to align himself with the Mashona and Manyika—whom he tends to regard as inferior—discouraged many otherwise willing recruits from applying.

As a consequence, towards the end of 1940 a platoon was sent to Matabeleland on a recruiting tour, journeying as far as Mphoengs on the Bechuanaland border. As many men as possible from the areas to be visited were included in the party, and after each parade the soldiers, smartly uniformed and evidently happy, were encouraged to mix freely with the crowd. This uncomplicated exercise in public relations proved a success, and increasing numbers of the Matablele applied to join the Regiment. It was not until March, 1941, however, when the Tribal Chiefs from Matabeleland were invited to inspect the Battalion at work in its completed camp that the libels were finally and absolutely discredited.

The majority of Africans who eventually found their way to Borrowdale Camp—often after long and difficult journeys from remote rural villages—were untouched by even the faintest veneer of sophistication. In consequence, they presented their instructors with unusual, and often bizarre, problems. The training cadre had to exercise extraordinary tact, patience and understanding in solving them. Furthermore an African, even if only semi-literate, could earn a far larger wage as a domestic servant than as a soldier; the proverbial (and in this instance, quite literal) King's Shilling was often regarded with disdain and indifference. The Regiment, therefore, had no alternative but to draw its first recruits from the tribal reserves. Many of these recruits had not even the rudiments of an education, and few had seen towns, trains or motor vehicles. Moreover, tribal custom tended to disrupt military discipline. It was not unusual, for example, to find some raw recruit being cosseted by his superiors, his most glaring faults overlooked, and discover that he was the son of some petty chief or headman. Another practice was stopped only with the greatest difficulty. The African tribal warrior is traditionally denied nothing by his less privileged clansmen. Cattle, women, goods—they are his by right, and what is not given freely he takes by force. Only by implementing the most rigid discipline was it finally driven home that the white King's soldiers did not have automatic rights to other people's property. Another failing of those early recruits was their inordinate lust for the pursuit of game. Old hands still recall the Battalion parade which turned into a riot when a hare rather foolishly chose to loiter on the edge of the parade-ground. With one accord, and with excited shrill whoops, the men broke ranks and gave chase, ignoring their cursing and shouting officers until the hare was finally caught. Tactfully, the incident was quietly forgotten.

But with infinite caution each problem was slowly overcome. It is to the very great credit of the original officers and N.C.O.s that within a relatively short time the Battalion was judged fit for active service. Those instructors built far more, however, than simply a competent fighting machine. They created an homogeneous family, and for its members—black and white, Mashona and Matabele— the Rhodesian African Rifles soon acquired the ethos and prestige of a tribe, with its own independent customs and discipline. Much of this feeling of unity was deliberately fostered by Colonel Wane, who emphasized the importance of participation by all ranks in the life of the Regiment. To this end the white officers and non-commissioned officers were required to live in single quarters in the Camp, and were allowed to visit their wives and families only twice a week. Dining-in nights were also held every Friday night in the Officers' Mess, although these were inevitably followed by pre-dawn route-marches on Saturday morning.

It was not, in fact, unusual to find an officer tottering out of the Mess at 2.00 a.m., hurriedly changing into his field service marching order, and parading at 3.00 a.m. for the start of the weekly route-march.

Initially, it had been intended to name the Battalion after its predecessor—the Rhodesian Native Regiment—but this proposal was eventually rejected. First, the word "native" was unpopular among the majority of Africans, and second, it was felt that the initials "R.N.R." had a nautical flavour inappropriate to land-locked Rhodesia. Over many years the King's African Rifles, one of whose Battalions had been raised and was stationed in Nyasaland, had built up an enviable and well-earned reputation. It was natural that, in casting round for a name for the new Battalion, the K.A.R. should be discussed, and it was not extraordinary that the final choice should be similar: the Rhodesian African Rifles.

During a period when German U-Boats dictated the movement of Allied shipping over most of the world's oceans, military clothing and equipment was often unobtainable in Rhodesia. The occasional consignments that did manage to get through the blockade were in heavy demand, and the Regiment fared badly in the general distribution. The African ranker's uniform consisted of a woollen jumper closed to the neck with four buttons, beneath a stiff collar, khaki shorts, puttees rolled from the top of the boots to just below the knee, and bush hats. The left brim of the hat was turned up, and on this the Regimental Badge was pinned. For the first few months the badge was merely a two-inch triangle of black cloth but later, from many designs submitted, the present badge was chosen—a Matabele shield upon which is laid a stabbing assegai and a Mashona spear, crossed, under a vertical knobkerrie. It was designed by Mr. A. Bayliss, a draughtsman in one of the Government departments, and the first badges were made by a jewellers' firm, Keays, of Salisbury.

(Mr. Bayliss' original sketch still hangs in the Officers' Mess at Methuen Barracks where the Regiment is now housed.) Officers wore the same uniform, except on ceremonial occasions, when they donned a bushjacket instead of the jersey. Since leather Sam Browne belts were not to be had at any price, an ordinary web belt, with one brace-strap in place of the cross-strap, was substituted.

By mid-July two full companies had been recruited and were in training. Mornings were given over to military duties, and the afternoons were spent erecting a camp, for until this had been done the only shelter was that provided by a belt of gum trees. Gradually the camp began to take shape. Under the direction of the Pioneer Branch of the B.S.A.P. neat rows of rondavels, constructed of mud-covered gum poles with thatch roofs, were built to provide homes for the askari. Not far from these a file of mud huts housed the European other ranks with, at one end, an elongated hut providing the Sergeants' Mess. Here a rather unique method of accounting was adopted which allowed any non-commissioned officer to help himself to drink from the stock-cupboard at will, requiring only that he put the requisite charge in a saucer provided for the purpose, helping himself to change if necessary. The method seems to have worked because the Mess made a consistently handsome profit. (Many years later this building was destined to become the venue for Courts Martial.) More squat huts were built to accommodate the officers, but the Officers' Mess—a brick building—was not built until 1941. Those who built Borrowdale Camp did so under the impression that it would not be required for a period of longer than two years. They were not to know that it would serve the Regiment for an additional twelve, and that it would not be until 1954 that the Rhodesian African Rifles would move to its present barracks near Bulawayo.

Chapter

2

Early Days

ON September 20, 1940, the first African Regimental
Sergeant-Major joined the Battalion. R.S.M.
Lechanda was an outstanding soldier. He had first
seen service as a boy-bugler with the King's African Rifles
in Somaliland at the age of ten. During the First World
War he had been awarded the Distinguished Conduct
Medal in East Africa for leading a patrol against a German
position, dispersing it, and inflicting casualties on the
enemy. He had also been awarded the Military Medal for
saving a large ration dump, which had been surrounded by
the enemy, from destruction. On this occasion, gathering
twelve askari at random, Lechanda had led an assault on a
German machine-gun post in which three guns had been
concentrated; he captured one gun and forced the others to
withdraw. Following up, his patrol then killed nine of the
enemy and captured four of their African carriers. Ever
afterwards, when asked about the incident, he would
explain ingenuously: "They came to steal our rations—
but we got the food they left behind instead."

Lechanda served with the Regiment until October 17,
1942, when, loyal to his own tradition, he died in the ranks
and surrounded by his comrades. As the Battalion was
returning to barracks from a route-march, the R.S.M.
stepped out of the column at the gates of St. George's
College on the Borrowdale Road and within a few minutes
died quietly by the roadside. He was buried the next day
with the entire Regiment following the coffin of a much
respected old soldier.

Though beset by logistical difficulties, the Battalion
gradually increased its stock of weapons and equipment.
Initially the men were armed with the P.14 rifle. Though a
reasonably good weapon it had two major defects—it was
not sturdy enough to withstand the often clumsy, and
always heavy, handling of the askari, and it had a weak
ejector mechanism which made jammed cartridges commonplace. Heavier fire-power was provided by obsolete Lewis
Guns (one of which was issued to each section). These were
replaced in 1942 by Bren Guns. A few Vickers machine-
guns were also obtained, together with some three-inch
mortars. Finally, in February 1941, a signal platoon was
formed, and by the end of that year the Secretary for
Defence was able to report:

> 'The Signal Platoon has shown satisfactory progress.
> The unit is fairly well equipped with signal equipment,
> and when pack wireless sets are received will be on a good
> operational basis. Some of the Africans have had experi-
> ence of wireless working, and show adaptability.'

Long route-marches characterised the early training of
the Regiment, and by 1941 it had gained a solid reputation
for being able to cover ground on foot very quickly indeed.
Colonel Wane had been among those who had had the
chastening experience of hunting von Lettow-Vorbeck in
small circles round East Africa, and he was determined that,
if the unit could do nothing else, it would at least be able
to march. He ordered therefore that two route-marches—
which were to total a distance of fifty miles—should be
completed every week. Wane himself often led these
long columns of singing, marching men, usually mounted
on a fine thoroughbred, but sometimes on foot. These
weekly marches culminated in 1941 with a major exercise
which the Secretary describes in his annual Report.

> 'On August 8 the unit commenced a tactical march to
> the eastern border of the Colony, returning to Salisbury
> on September 11.'

In the event, this laconic description is somewhat under-stated. The "Tactical March" in fact began with a summons one morning for the Battalion second-in-command, Major Wells (commanding during Wane's temporary absence) to report to Defence Headquarters. Here he was advised that the Regiment was to march to Umtali and back (a distance of some 360 miles), engaging in at least two major exercises each day. Major Wells was also ordered, incidentally, to submit his completed plan of action by 4.00 p.m. that same day, but very sensibly made no attempt to comply with this unreasonable request.

To make the operation more realistic, the Rhodesian Armoured Car Regiment—then stationed at Umtali—were subpoenaed to provide an enemy *en route*. This they did effectively, despite the fact that, in the light-hearted "war" which developed, they sustained two setbacks. On the first occasion an armoured car rushed a barbed-wire entanglement in order to prove "how ineffectual" it was. Although, it must be admitted, the vehicle did eventually manage to breach the barrier, it took the crew four days of hard work to unravel the tangle of wire which adorned it. During another engagement, the Officer Commanding the armour foolishly pushed his head through his turret only to have it crowned by a large and over-ripe "kaffir orange" which the askari were using in lieu of molotov-cocktails. On the return march, the last leg of the journey—from Marandellas to the Camp—was completed as a race between Companies. The winning Company covered the 40·5 miles in eleven hours and fifty-eight minutes, despite the fact that the rules stipulated that each Company must cook and eat a hot meal on the way.

In the same Report, the Secretary also commented:

'As a result of the decision to retain this unit in the Colony, opportunity has been presented for further periods of training to be carried out.'

Again, much has been left unsaid. With the new year had come a restless demand from all ranks of the Regiment for posting to an active theatre of war. Officers and men were growing bored and frequent "false alarms" did not improve the situation. On several occasions the Battalion was ordered to prepare for a transfer, and embarkation leave was granted, but each time the men returned to camp they were told that the posting had been cancelled. One officer became so frustrated by this continuous wavering that he retired to his bed and refused to leave it for several days. Other officers applied for postings to more active units, and others eased their irritations by turning mess nights into minor riots. As for the askari—they simply downed tools and "went home". Or else they indulged in petty crime. During 1941 almost 3,500 minor offences were punished by unit commanders, and this figure was to rise to staggering heights before the Battalion finally received its marching orders.

The Government, though sympathetic, couldn't help. Apart from being unable to meet the cost of equipping the Rhodesian African Rifles to the same standard as other active units, the regiment was still needed in the country. One of the main arguments for forming the Battalion had been the need to safeguard the internal security of the Colony, and until a satisfactory substitute could be found, the Government rightly refused to compromise.

To provide this substitute, and also to ensure a steady stream of recruits for the Regiment, it was decided to form a Depot Unit, to be known as "The Rhodesian African Rifles Depot". Major Jack Peel-Nelson was recalled from West Africa to organise and command the unit, and it was opened on July 3, 1941, with an authorised establishment of 400. It had been found that the system of training recruits within the Battalion was far from satisfactory, and the new Depot—situated just opposite Borrowdale Camp—allowed for a continuity of training which had been evidently lacking so far. There was an immediate rush of recruits to join and the Depot was launched in a blaze of publicity. One local African newspaper ended an article on the new venture with the following advice to would-be soldiers:

'Any of you who have friends joining, or wishing to join, the Rhodesian African Rifles, must ask them to practise closing their left eye and keeping their right eye open, as it is necessary for the firing of a rifle. It would save considerable time if recruits were able to do this when they apply for enlistment.'

Wise counsel too, for it was remarkable how few of the new recruits seemed able to perform this apparently simple feat.

Meanwhile, it became obvious that members of the Regiment had felt no hesitation in airing their grievances about "home duties" in every possible quarter, and on September 16, at a farewell parade given in his honour, the retiring Governor, Sir Herbert Stanley, administered a gentle admonishment.

'I am well aware that you have all been hoping for the day when you would be summoned to go forth from here and take your place in the firing line: I sympathise with you in your great disappointment that these hopes have not yet been fulfilled. I think I may say that the authorities with whom rests the decision as to the movement of troops in East Africa, West Africa, and the Middle East, know that in the Rhodesian African Rifles there is available good material: well trained and eager to answer any call.

I am confident if and when the need for further African infantry units arises in any of those theatres of war you will not be overlooked. Meanwhile it behoves you, as good soldiers, to keep yourselves fit and ready. Your marching orders may come at any time. That will depend on events outside the borders of Southern Rhodesia, events beyond the control of the Government of Rhodesia. When you get your chance—as I hope you will—I know that you will give a good account of yourselves.'

At the beginning of 1942 the Government's Defence Policy underwent a major change. They were finding increasing difficulty in fulfilling their manpower commitments, and to ease the strain they decided to implement a policy of "Africanisation". Basically, this meant that African soldiers were to be trained to take over certain tasks from their European counterparts in a number of units stationed in the country. Chief amongst those to be replaced would be signallers, cooks and drivers. It was hoped that this action would release more European soldiers for posting to active fronts. Those units principally affected were:

> 1st and 2nd Bns, The Rhodesia Regiment
> The S.R. Reconnaissance Regiment
> The S.R. Signal (Depot) Unit
> The S.R. (Motorised) Field Ambulance

In order to facilitate this transition, a Driving and Maintenance School was established at the R.A.R. Depot and recruiting was speeded up. It was estimated that if the Africanisation policy was to be fully implemented a further 800 Africans would have to be recruited, in addition to maintaining the prevailing establishments at full strength. The Depot, which had up until then been rather neglected, now suddenly found itself the centre of a storm of activity. Depot's primary task had been the training of recruits for the Battalion: men who had completed their course and were waiting absorption into the Regiment being used to provide guard details at Defence Headquarters and at vehicle parks of the territorial battalions. Africanisation, however, envisaged a tremendous broadening of Depot's functions, to the extent that ultimately it should become the general training centre for all African personnel. It became, therefore, a matter of urgency that the camp receive some long-overdue attention—principally from the Department of Works. The huts, which were starting to show signs of wear and tear, were re-thatched and plastered, and a considerable amount of new construction was started including alterations to the Officers' Mess, additional latrines, a laundry, and a de-lousing plant!

In an effort to ease the frustration and tedium of home duties, the Battalion training programme was given a stimulus. Italian internees were then being sent to South Africa from Abyssinia and Somaliland. It was arranged between the two Governments that a number of Italians should be dispatched to Rhodesian internment camps, and the Battalion was given the task of collecting the prisoners from Durban and escorting them to their new homes. These trips were to take place periodically throughout 1942, the first of them in January. One of the officers recalls some of the highlights of this particular journey:

'Late in January we left Salisbury by train for Durban. After marching from Borrowdale Camp we entrained: six to a compartment. Officers and non-commissioned officers messed in the dining-car, and the troops had their meals served to them in their compartments. The journey down was without incident as far as Johannesburg, where we changed to an electric train for the final stage to Durban. This was a new experience for the Africans, who couldn't understand how the train moved without an engine. It was during this journey, too, that the troops first saw the banana plantations of Natal, and were so impressed by the sight that they made up the song which was later to become the Regimental March.

We detrained at Clairwood, a short distance from Durban, and marched to Clairwood Camp—a large tented establishment which, because it was pitched on sand, was fairly uncomfortable. The stuff seemed to get into everything and everywhere. However, we were compensated by the evenings, which were made memorable by an Italian band, captured with their instruments in the Western Desert, who played for us in the Officers' Mess. They even had a soloist—an Italian pilot who, having been shot down and had saved himself by parachuting to safety, wore the caterpillar badge. He was a wonderful tenor, and when he sung "O Sole Mio" it brought a lump into every throat.

Clairwood also contained at that time a number of Indian Naval Officers who messed with us, and certain British Army units on their way to the Far East. Many of these latter were destined to be captured by the Japanese at the fall of Singapore.

Many of the askari saw the sea for the first time when we were taken to Durban North Beach for a swim. There were loud exclamations at the saltiness of the water. Early one morning we entrained for Durban Docks to collect the first batch of internees which had been brought there by the giant Dutch troopship, *Amsterdam*. Our troops, more used to the canoes and yachts of our small lakes, could hardly believe that such a huge ship could be supported on water. We had no trouble with the internees, who were quickly escorted back to Clairwood, de-loused, and put into the prisoners' cage until our return trip to Rhodesia.

This was uneventful, and there were no attempted escapes, though we noticed that the platform at Johannesburg was fairly bristling with machine-guns. The Italians were taken to internment camps at Gatooma, Fort Victoria and Umvuma, and were guarded at these places by the Battalion until a Corps specially formed for the purpose took over. Many of the internees were later released on parole to work on local farms, and proved very useful.'

Unfortunately, these new adventures provided trouble-makers with fresh material for rumours aimed at degrading the Regiment. It soon became general gossip that the askari had been sent into South Africa without the consent of that Government and as a result had been stopped at Mafeking, ordered off the train, and disarmed—their rifles being replaced by pickhandles—whereupon the men had mutinied. This, of course, was nonsense and the allegations were vigorously denied by Sir Godfrey Huggins in the Legislative Assembly. But, regrettably, his speech did not put an end to the matter. Certain local farmers chose this moment to write to the newspapers suggesting that the

askari might be usefully employed in shooting out tribes
of baboons which were eating their crops. To the askari, the
idea that he, a soldier, should be asked to "fight" baboons
was a sharp blow to his dignity. Allied to the allegation of
mutiny, this suggestion provoked a fit of mass sullen anger
throughout the Regiment which turned into flaring rage
when soldiers of the Rhodesian Air Askari Corps—the
Colony's other African regiment—started to indulge in a
little gentle leg-pulling. Friendly rivalry turned into
belligerent animosity, and brawls became standard practice
whenever members of the two regiments met, resulting
in disciplinary patrols under European command and the
banning of local African townships to both. Luckily this
enmity died down almost as quickly as it had flared up, and
friendly relations were soon resumed.

During 1942, the Battalion provided "enemy" and
demonstration troops for the annual territorial exercises.
The territorials were not the only ones to benefit from
these exercises, for the standard of training in the Battalion
rose considerably. It was during one of these exercises—on
August 19—that two young officers earned commendations
in Force Orders for courageous action. Units of the
Regiment were engaged in an amphibious assault across the
Hunyani River when one of the boats carrying Lieutenant
George Barlow and six African soldiers suddenly capsized a
few yards from the bank. Barlow and five of the askari
managed to scramble ashore, but the sixth remained with
the boat, which now drifted into midstream. Within a few
minutes the man, weighed down by his heavy equipment,
lost his grip and sank. Immediately Barlow and Lieutenant
Inskipp (who had been superintending the exercise) both
also carrying full packs, plunged in and after a struggle
brought the half-drowned soldier to safety.

It was about this time, when both Battalion and Depot
appeared to be gradually acquiring the respectability of
permanence, that a new status-symbol appeared—a

Regimental Band. There are as many versions of how the Band was conceived as there are persons who claim the responsibility for its conception. It seems, however, that the originator was almost certainly Major Peel Nelson. Having a remarkable talent for music himself—which often found an outlet on Mess Nights when, accompanying himself on the banjo, he entertained his brother officers with a wide-ranging selection of the less respectable favourites—he decided to form a bugle band in an attempt to improve his recruits' parade drill. The first official mention of the band is found in the Defence Report for 1941; "The bugle band is progressing favourably. The personnel are improving as instrumentalists and should form a good nucleus for a brass band which is to be formed later." Despite the Secretary's ever-optimistic predictions several months passed before a bandmaster and a stock of ancient instruments could be located. Mr. Harley Brims, formerly a bandsman aboard the Royal Yacht, was discovered serving in the Military Police in Bulawayo, and was posted to the Regiment. He was to prove invaluable, especially in the help and advice he gave in publishing the Regimental March. The African has a natural harmony and will break into song on every possible occasion, although the songs are often only a repetitive musical account of whatever happens to be of most interest to the individual at that particular moment. Route marches, therefore, often provided a melodious diary of the previous week's social activities. But one particular song was widely popular— "Sweet Bananas"—whose verses were based on the sights and experiences of the troops during their train journeys through Natal. Under Mr. Brims' direction this air was transcribed and forwarded to the Royal College of Music, Kneller Hall. The Regiment offered a prize of £25 to the pupil who produced the best arrangement based on this, and in due course a complete orchestration arrived.

Internee-escorting, exercises and the new broadening of

the Battalion's activities, interesting though they were, did little to quell the intensifying demand for a more active posting. The officers displayed their restlessness in a rather unusual way. When the Commander, Southern Rhodesia Forces, was asked to address them on the subject he was treated to a hectic half-hour during which it was made very clear to him that the Regiment considered they were being most unfairly treated. Some little time later the Prime Minister himself was placed in the "hot seat" at a repeat performance. The askari's boredom with this enforced period of repetitive training was reflected in the disciplinary statistics of 1943. They show that there was a marked increase in minor offences, in fact some 6,500 petty violations of military discipline were recorded for that year; at the same time a comparatively large number of discharge applications were received from the askari—sixty-six in 1943. Even this figure is not a true indication of the restlessness of the askari, for many simply discharged themselves of their own volition, preferring to pack up and go home rather than involve themselves in the fuss and bother of a more formal departure.

Matters had reached a critical stage when the authorities at last decided that circumstances permitted fresh posting for the Regiment; in the first instance to East Africa, and thereafter as required by East Africa Command. The Regiment were probably not aware how much of their gratitude for that decision they owed to Brigadier W. A. Dimoline who had expressed a strong wish to have them in his command—the 28th (East African) Independent Infantry Brigade. But the soldiers of the Rhodesian African Rifles were not destined to hear of their good fortune until August 14 when the Governor, Sir Evelyn Baring, inspecting the Battalion at Borrowdale Camp, addressed the Parade. He began,

'Officers, non-commissioned officers and other ranks of the Rhodesian African Rifles: You are about to leave

3 24 pp.

Southern Rhodesia to fight for the King, who needs every loyal citizen to help to win this war . . . .'

It is doubtful that the remainder of his speech was heard. The announcement came as a complete surprise and, after weary months of frustrating delay, it brought loud relief and elation.

As if to compensate for their earlier tardiness, Defence Headquarters now began to move with unaccustomed speed. Staff Officers from East Africa Command visited Rhodesia to conclude arrangements, and from their reports it became obvious that the original estimate of requisite personnel had been far too low. In order to bring the Battalion and first-line reinforcements up to the desired strength the policy of Africanisation had to be reversed. Native troops were withdrawn from units which had already started to implement Africanisation and posted back to the Battalion. To ensure that the Regiment would not be stranded without trained replacements while on active service, instruction at the Depot was accelerated. At the same time, a second Battalion was formed, and accommodated in a new camp built on the opposite side of the road, while recruiting in Matabeleland was stimulated by a new depot hastily built in Bulawayo.

As the moment of embarkation drew nearer men were granted leave. There was a great deal of private speculation about how many of them—now that active service was imminent—would return. The speculations were unfounded. In fact, many of the askari, fearing that they might be left behind, came back before their leave had expired. A further military phenomenon was observed when large numbers of deserters returned voluntarily pleading that they had left in protest against the never-ending training, and were now ready to take their punishment providing it would be over in time for them to accompany the Regiment to East Africa.

Chapter
3
East Africa and Ceylon

THE Advance Party, consisting of three Europeans
and twenty Africans, left Salisbury on November
12, 1943, followed shortly by the remainder of the
Battalion—sixty Europeans and 840 Africans—in three
drafts leaving on November 17, 19, and 24. A final
draft of reinforcements left on December 30, arriving in
Nairobi on January 27, 1944. These dates are found in the
Report to the Legislative Assembly for 1943 and when
collated with other sources appear to be correct, but the
Secretary's Annual Report is not always completely
trustworthy. The same report, for example, states that a
party of four Europeans and 136 Africans from the Regiment left Salisbury on April 1 to escort a batch of internees
to Durban. No record of their return, however, was ever
made, and to all intents they may still be languishing on the
Natal coast.

The drafts travelled overland on a variety of transport—
from Salisbury to Kamina by train, then to Kabalo in the
Congo by lorry, again by train to Albertville on the western
shores of Lake Tanganyika, crossing to Kigoma in Tanganyika by ferry. Then another train journey to Mwanza
on the southern tip of Lake Victoria, and ferry to Kisuma
on the north-eastern shores, where they again entrained
for the final stretch to Nairobi. The third draft varied the
route slightly by calling at Elisabethville instead of Albertville, where a lone and somewhat bewildered askari informed them that he had been accidentally separated from
his friends in the previous draft and had missed the ferry.

Each draft, as it arrived in Nairobi, was met by Colonel N. S. Ferris, O.B.E., T.D., the Southern Rhodesia Liaison Officer, who was to be their link with home during their stay in East Africa. Apart from the Regiment, there were also stationed in East Africa at the time some 600 Rhodesians of all ranks, and Colonel Ferris was a very busy man indeed.

After the official welcome, each draft marched to Ngong some miles south of Nairobi, where they were to begin their preliminary training. Here they spent Christmas 1943, amply catered for by various charitable organisations in Rhodesia. Each askari received a special gift that Christmas: a card from the King and Queen bearing on one side a portrait of Their Majesties, and on the other a message into which each man's name and Regimental Number had been inserted.

By the end of 1943 the Battalion had been re-equipped, most particularly with the new ·303 rifle. Although grateful for this vastly superior weapon, the askari felt cheated on the bayonet, for they much preferred the awesome sword-length blade of the old type to the six-inch steel of the new issue. On the last day of the year the Battalion was inspected by General Sir William Platt, General Officer Commanding East Africa Command. Impressed by the standard of training, he authorised advanced instruction and accordingly the Regiment left Ngong early in January and settled at Embakasi. They spent three days—from the 12th to 14th January—on the Athi Plains engaged in a number of Battalion exercises and on the 15th they again moved, this time to an established military camp at Yatta. Their stay here was short, and on the 27th they moved to Moshi at the foot of Mount Kilimanjaro, where they set up a base camp. At Moshi they were finally joined by the last draft of reinforcements from Rhodesia.

February was spent in an attempt to familiarise the men with jungle fighting. A series of exercises were held on the

Sanya Plains, at the foot of Mount Meru, where the Rhodesians found themselves in a terrain that bore little resemblance to the mopani bush and thorn scrub of home. The Menu heights were covered with thick forest and bamboo jungle and the foothills were notched with deep gorges and ravines. Although the area bore little similarity to the Burmese jungle, it provided, at least, better preparation for the coming fight than anything that could have been found in Rhodesia.

During March the Battalion was again on the move, bound for Kirua, where they completed a jungle course, and at the end of the month they left for Hump, where they were to take part in field-firing exercises. On arrival they found the place to be little better than a swamp and quite unsuitable. Three armoured carriers had been issued to the Regiment at Yatta and they now received a further seven. Fearsome, clanking monsters—often driven with more zest than skill—they were a permanent source of danger and amusement to all.

Although Nairobi was no longer the operational base it had been at the beginning of the war, it was still the headquarters of East Africa Command, responsible for units in Ceylon and Burma, Italian Somaliland and Eastern Abyssinia, Madagascar and other islands in the Indian Ocean. As such it was a bustling, active city, its streets thronging with thousands of soldiers from many parts of the world. The officers and men of the Regiment found little complaint with the diversions offered during their occasional spells of leave. The askari, many of whom had never before been beyond the borders of Rhodesia, could hardly credit the strange new sights and customs they now experienced. (Later, in Ceylon and Burma, their amazement knew no bounds, and their letters home were filled with incredulous astonishment.) Some of the Europeans, too, found difficulty in adjusting to the new circumstances. One of these, the popular R.M.O., Doctor Jim Kennedy (who was afterwards to dedicate his life to the service of the African in Rhodesia) was involved in an incident which, though entertaining in retrospect, was not amusing at the time. While on an exercise one day he came across a group of Masai warriors apparently trying to slaughter one of their cattle. Dr. Kennedy, who was inordinately fond of animals, was horrified to see the beast struggling and kicking, bellowing in obvious pain. Thinking the young men were making a botch of the job, he pulled out his revolver and, before anyone could stop him, promptly shot it dead. The Masai, notoriously sensitive people when it comes to cattle, were furious, and during the ensuing row the kindly Doctor learnt that he had seriously misjudged the situation. The young men had simply been drawing their mid-day meal of blood from the animal's jugular vein—a long established staple of the Masai diet. Dr. Kennedy was given a long lecture by the local District Commissioner and fined fifteen pounds. Nevertheless, he was fortunate; the Masai have been known to settle arguments about cattle with their razor-sharp spears.

At the end of April the R.A.R. was informed that officers and European other ranks over the age of thirty-eight would not be allowed to accompany the Battalion in the event of posting to Burma. This was cruel news. A number of men who had been with the Regiment from the start had to be replaced. The changes took place during August, the Commanding Officer being among those to suffer. Lieutenant Colonel MacDonald, who had taken over from Wane, was succeeded by Lieutenant Colonel G. W. H. Goode of the Queen's Royal Regiment (West Surrey). Although a regular soldier in the British Army, Colonel Goode was also the son of a former Chief Secretary of Northern Rhodesia and was readily accepted by the Regiment. The other replacements all came from Rhodesia with the exception of the Quartermaster (Royal Norfolk Regiment) and the Field Works Officer (West Yorkshire

Regiment). By the end of this shakedown the Companies were commanded as follows:

> Major C. S. Davies—"A" Company
> Major R. Lowings—"B" Company
> Major R. Stirrup—"C" Company
> Major S. Morris—"D" Company

The new Battalion second-in-command was Major W. Walker.

In May, the camp at Moshi was visited by an anti-malarial squad who confirmed the long-held (and often vocal) suspicions of the Rhodesians by pronouncing it "unfit for human habitation". Though the Battalion did not realise it, this ritual was an annual performance, as was the subsequent conference called to discuss the matter at Force Headquarters in Nairobi, and as was the decision reached at the conference—the Battalion would remain where it was.

On May 12, Brigadier E. R. Day, C.B.E., Commander Military Forces Southern Rhodesia, visited the Battalion and was bombarded with questions on future policy, the future of axed officers, and above all when the Regiment was to be employed in a forward area. The landings in Normandy were about to take place, the whole tempo of the war was quickening, and the Rhodesians were beginning to feel that they had been passed by without even catching a glimpse of the enemy. They did not know it but the moment of encounter was fast approaching. The 22nd (East African) Brigade stationed in Ceylon was about to lose one of its battalions and it had been decided to fill the gap with the R.A.R.

The Regiment was ordered to leave Moshi on June 20 and take part in a nine-day exercise (code-named *John Peel*) which had been devised to screen the movement of the troops to the coast *en route* for Ceylon. The Battalion completed the first phase of the exercise, an eighty-mile

advance to Arusha, in four days, with local actions against
small parties of "Japanese" (provided by the Northern
Rhodesia Regiment) being fought all the way. As usual, this
rapid advance confused the Umpires, who had counted on
the dense vegetation, coupled with an abnormal heat, to
slow down the Battalion. The climax of the advance was
to be an attack on Arusha itself which, according to plan,
was to be initiated at dawn. After a difficult approach, the
Battalion settled down in a swampy banana grove some
four miles from the town and prepared for the final assault.
This involved making an approach march to the town and
an attack at first light, supported by the armoured carriers.
Soon after midnight, on a dark and moonless night, the men
set off in single file. But at dawn it was discovered that, with
the exception of "A" Company, elements of Battalion Headquarters, and the Adjutant, Captain Ted Goddard, who
were all in the correct position, nobody else was in sight.
Major Davies, commanding "A" Company, thought he had
better try to find his Commanding Officer and ordered his
signaller to contact Battalion Headquarters. Battalion
Headquarters' signaller, however, was among those who
had managed to find the rendezvous, and Major Davies
spent a merry five minutes rushing back and forth between
the two wireless sets talking to himself before he realised
what had happened. Eventually he decided to lead the
final assault personally and only narrowly avoided an armed
clash between his askari and units of Somali troops who
were guarding Arusha and thought they were being attacked
in earnest. Just as this misunderstanding was being sorted
out there was a great roaring of engines, and the armoured
carriers—which everyone had forgotten about—came
clanking out of the bush. Captain George Hartley, in the
lead carrier, seeing that he was about to mow down un-
countable numbers of soldiers, ordered his African driver
to brake. This unfortunate, forgetting in his panic that
there are two brakes, applied only one, with the result

An askari of the R.A.R.—a painting which now hangs in the Regimental Headquarters.

Rhodesian African Rifles

Bantu Mirror —————⟶ 30 8 41

African recruits are required for the above Regiment.

Those who wish to serve their KING should apply to the nearest Native Commissioner's Office where particulars of service can be obtained and tickets for the journey to Salisbury issued to those who are passed as medically fit.

Rates of pay are as under :—

	Per Diem
Regimental Sergeant/Major	2/-
Enlisted Native School Master	2/-
Company Sergeant/Major	1/8
Enlisted Native Clerk	1/8
Sergeant	1/4
Corporal	1/2
Lance Corporal	1/1.
Soldier	1/-

Conditions of Service also include free clothing, rations and quarters.

Commanding this Regiment is Lt. Col. Wane (Msoro-we-gomo) who is known to most Africans in Southern Rhodesia.

Abantu bayafuneka ukungena ubusoja e Rhodesian African Rifles.

Labo abafuna ukusebenzela uKing wabo kababuze kusi Komitshi esise duze labo, nguye ozabaxoxela konke okwenziwayo futi nguye ozabapa amatikiti okukwelisa isitimela ukuya eSalisbury. Inzuzo eyalungiselwa ukupa umuntu mayelana lokwazi kwenqondo yake injengaloku :—

URegimental Sgt/Major	2/-	nge langa
Ongena eyi Native School Master	2/-	nge langa
Company Sgt/Major	1/8	nge langa
Lowo ongena eyi Native Clerk	1/8	nge langa
Sergeant	1/4	nge langa
Corporal	1/2	nge langa
Lance Corporal	1/3	nge langa
uMsoja	1/-	nge langa

Izigqoko, ukudhla lendawo yokulala akubadalelwa. U Lt. Col. Wane waziwa ngabantu ngegama lokuti Msorowegomo e Southern Rhodesia nguye ogcina amasoja.

Vanu varikudikanwa kupinda uSoja mu Rhodesian African Rifles.

Avo vanoda kubata basa ra King wavo vabvunze kwa Native Commissioner ari pedjgo navo kuti avatsanangurire maitiro ebasa ravo nekupiwa matikiti ekukwirisa chitima kuyenda ku Salisbury.

Mubairo wakagadzirwa kupa munhu kuyenzanisa nekuziva kwake zwakadai :—

Regimental Sgt/Major	2/-	pa dzuva
Anopinda ari Native School Master	2/-	pa dzuva
Company Sgt/Major	1/8	pa dzuva
Anopinda ari Native Clerk	1/8	pa dzuva
Sergeant	1/4	pa dzuva
Corporal	1/2	pa dzuva
Lance Corporal	1/3	pa dzuva
Musoja	1/-	pa dzuva

Zwokupfeka, zwokudjga, nenzwimbo yekurinda pachena. Vanochengeta masoja ndi Lt. Col. Wane (Msorowegomo) anozivikanwa kwazwo kuvanu vazhinji vemu Southern Rhodesia.

The original advertisement calling for recruits. Published in the Bantu Mirror *on the 30th August, 1941, in English, Sindebele, and Shona.*

Parading in front of their quarters at the Borrowdale Camp, during the early stages of construction.

"A" Company—making their first public appearance—march through the Salisbury African township on 11th November, 1941.

that the vehicle spun round like a top about half a dozen times before charging off in the opposite direction. For some strange reason, the only official comment on the whole sad affair by General Platt appears to have been a complaint that the men were unshaven and failed to salute him when he passed the returning column later that morning in his staff car.

From Arusha the Regiment moved to Yatta and from there, on September 4, to Nairobi where it entrained for Mombasa. During the afternoon of the 5th they boarded the troopship *Strathaven* in Mombasa harbour. The askari were greatly excited and letters home were full of wonder at this strange new mode of travel:

> 'The sea is an enormous place, nothing but water. Wherever we look we see just water, which is very salty. I had seen the sea once before at Durban, but I never knew there was so much of it. Our ship was very large, just like a small town; passages that seemed as long as streets, and hundreds of little rooms and halls—like the big hotels in Rhodesia. On the big sea most people get sick, it is called "sea-sickness," but it is much worse than that. It lasts only a few days and most of us had this sea-sickness. At first we thought we should surely die, but we did not, and after two or three days we got better, and then how well we felt. Do you believe me when I tell you that we saw fish that fly? It is true. Yes, you may think that the stories we tell you of strange people, crocodiles, elephants that work, and flying fish are just big lies, but it's the honest truth. At night, whilst we travelled on that big ship, the little windows on the sides were closed so that enemy boats would not be able to see us. It was very hot on that journey and I was glad to get off the ship at Ceylon.'

The Rhodesians landed at Colombo on September 14, and immediately moved to Horana Camp where the 22nd East African Brigade was located. In addition to the normal support units, the Brigade consisted of 1st Battalion, The King's African Rifles, 3rd Battalion, The Northern

Rhodesia Regiment, and 1st Battalion, The Rhodesian African Rifles. In Ceylon, the 22nd functioned as a reserve unit used to supply bulk reinforcements to the 11th (East African) Division operating in Burma. The Brigade spent its time training officers and men to that end, with special emphasis on the techniques of jungle fighting. Officers were also trained to shoot an artillery battery in support of ground troops. It was generally agreed, however, that Ceylon was not really suited to this task, and Major W. Walker later wrote of the conditions there:

'The techniques of working in the jungle-covered hills of Ceylon bore little resemblance, as it transpired, to the problems which faced men later on the razor-edged ridges of the Arakan with their endless covering of dense bamboo. Men could not foresee the unbelievable difficulty of map reading in that featureless tangle of stems through which the Brigade fought later on, nor the problem of obtaining observed artillery support from the summit of features where visibility seldom exceeded twenty yards. In this respect training proved inadequate, and knowledge was bought later at the cost of experience.'

But the askari were thoroughly enjoying their new surroundings;

'How interesting our training was. We felt that we were really good soldiers when we had finished that work. We used live bullets. Big shells (as the huge bullets are called) fell near us; but it is strange that, although little pieces of the shells scratched us, we felt no fear, for we had become used to those happenings. We practised attacking places, just as though the enemy was hiding there. Running forward with hand-grenades (little bombs which are not as large as oranges) we threw them into holes and places where the enemy might be hiding, and then you should have seen what a mess those grenades made of the holes. If an enemy had been there before we threw the grenades he would certainly have been hard to find after the grenades had exploded. It is very exciting to fire rifles and Bren-guns at the enemy. We had only one accident. Private Wachekwa (1920) who came from Urungwe District was killed through a Bren-gun having a broken part. We buried him amongst the graves of other soldiers in a fine cemetery overlooking the Indian Ocean. Some of the soil from his grave was sent to his relatives in Rhodesia.'

Soon after the Regiment's arrival in Ceylon a training company was formed to accommodate the fresh reinforcements which arrived sporadically from Rhodesia. This company was to comprise the "fourth platoon" of each infantry company, and during the remainder of the campaign travelled with Brigade Headquarters providing guard and labour details. This procedure was not normal, but its advantages over the usual system of withholding reserves far in the rear were soon proved. Whereas the Regiment was able to replace casualties within a few hours, and with troops aware of the tactical situation, other units had to wait days—sometimes weeks—for reinforcements that arrived disoriented and bewildered.

By October the Battalion had become acclimatised to the steamy jungles of Ceylon and, in a two-day exercise near Hambanota, had been judged fit for duty in Burma. Some Brigade officers were detached to serve with battalions already engaged with the enemy, and the remainder—together with senior non-commissioned officers—attended local battle schools. On November 15, Lord Louis Mountbatten, Supreme Allied Commander South-East Asia, inspected the Brigade at Horana. He confirmed the fast-growing rumour that it would shortly be re-assigned, and brought the news that the East Africans would soon be required for operations with the 81st (West African) Division in the Arakan. Orders were received in due course and, after a brief postponement, the Brigade embarked at Colombo on December 2, not knowing their immediate destination, but well satisfied that they were at last on their way to the Front. On this occasion the men of the Battalion had their first experience of landing-craft, for these awkward

vehicles conveyed them from the pier to the troopship
Aronda. Early next morning they set sail in convoy with
troopships carrying the King's African Rifles and the
Northern Rhodesians, and escorted by two frigates. The
askari, experienced travellers by now, seemed to enjoy
their second sea voyage more than the first.

> 'The sea was very nice and quiet, but even so all of us
> soldiers kept watching each other, and when a man would
> walk to the side of the ship we would watch him and smile,
> and say to each other: *Wona, tarira, a chi ri ku rutsa!*
> [Look out. He is still vomiting], but there was no fun
> because nobody became sea-sick on this journey.
>
> Our big boat was not able to come close to the land,
> therefore we soldiers were carried out to the large ship
> in little boats. We were shown places where we were to
> sleep and where we would have our meals given to us.
> Our cooks at once became busy preparing a good dinner
> for us.
>
> We travelled happily for a whole week on the ship.
> One morning we wakened to find ourselves travelling
> very slowly towards a big river. Then it stopped and we
> climbed down into small boats again. These boats carried
> us right up the beautiful river, and then we landed. We
> were told that we were still in India.'

It was December 10, 1944; the East Africans had arrived
at Chittagong.

Chapter
4
Burma—1945

T HE Battle—or battles—for Burma involved many
hundreds of thousands of men over a period of
many, weary years. The Rhodesian African Rifles
arrived as the operation was already drawing to a close
and played, compared to more seasoned units, a relatively
small role. Small though it was, their part was vital, and
one not easily minimised. Although these chapters are
concerned mainly with those theatres and operations in
which the Regiment fought, its function in the Arakan can
best be seen against the perspective of the Burma campaign
as a whole.

The third, and final, Arakan Campaign had started
before the arrival of the Rhodesian African Rifles, but by
the time it ended the Regiment had taken its place in the
van of the advance. But, in truth, the Arakan Campaign
was itself of minor importance, and while the askari chopped
and inched his way through the bamboo jungles around
Taungup the decisive battles were being fought many
miles to the east.

In February, 1945, the Fourteenth Army, under Sir
William Slim, was making its historic push south through
Central Burma. Simultaneously, the Northern Combat
Area Command—a combined American/Chinese force—
was pressing the Japanese from the north-east. In the
narrow western coastal strip known as the Arakan, the 15th
Indian Corps was harassing the enemy. These encircling
forces, daily drawing the noose tighter, did not appear to
alarm the Japanese unduly. General Kimura, Commander-
in-Chief of the Japanese forces in Burma, believed that the

34

Map A

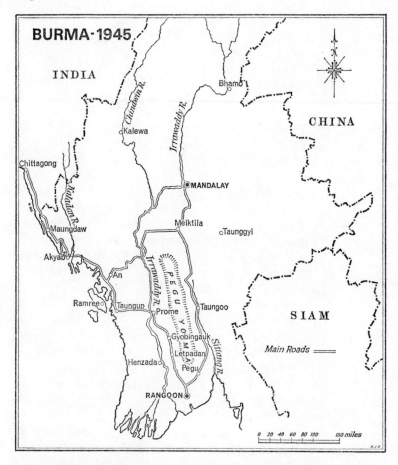

Fourteenth Army—divided as it was by the wide Irrawaddy River—could be checked and defeated in one decisive battle and he chose to stage the confrontation at Mandalay. His immediate aim was to collect here the largest available force as quickly as possible—a decision which involved withdrawing the majority of his units from every other Burmese front. The Japanese 54th Division, together with some units of the 55th, were then in the Arakan, and were among those instructed to fall back. But two strategic points in the Arakan were to remain in Japanese hands, for Kimura had no intention of leaving his back door open, inviting an attack from the rear by the 15th Corps. He reasoned that however large the Allied build-up might be in the coastal strip, their effectiveness would be neutralised if the two passes into the Irrawaddy Valley—at An and Taungup—were controlled by the Japanese.

At about this time the situation in the Arakan was also causing concern to the Allies. For some months a much smaller Japanese force had, merely by the implicit threat of its presence, required the virtually static occupation of four divisions (the 15th Corps) which could have been used with greater benefit elsewhere. Therefore, and not knowing that Kimura was in the process of withdrawing his units, the Allies initiated a more aggressive role which they hoped would resolve an unsatisfactory *status quo*.

Lieutenant-General Sir Phillip Christison, commanding the 15th, was ordered to make a limited advance in the area. Supported by 224 Group, Royal Air Force, his task was to force the Japanese from the coastal area, making it impossible for them to re-stage an offensive in the northern Arakan, and to secure forward airfields for supplying the Fourteenth Army's main drive to the east. Christison had under his command the 25th and 26th Indian Divisions, the 81st and 82nd West African Divisions, together with 3 Commando Brigade, and 50 Indian Tank Brigade. Opposing him, Lieutenant-General Sakurai Seizo commanded the Twenty-Eighth Army which, in the Arakan, had a regiment of the 54th Division and units of the 55th.

The topography of the area would have given any commander nightmares. It would be difficult to over-state the denseness of the Arakan vegetation, and the obstacle it offered to movement. A thick tangle of jungle crowded

close to bamboo-covered hills which rose steeply from the
mangrove swamps at the coast to the high Arakan Yomas
proper. Centuries of wind and rain had honed these hills
to knife-edges, and they were scarred and furrowed by a
network of watercourses known as *chaungs*. The gradient
of the slopes (often so steep that a foothold would be hard
to find), the razor-edged ridges surmounting them, and the
extreme density of the bamboo, were of the greatest tactical
importance. Advances had to be made on existing roads and
tracks (often leading into enemy ambushes) or new ones
had to be cut. Defensive emplacements, plans of attack,
every inch of forward movement, was limited by two
irreducible constraints—the hills and the jungle. Visibility
in the bamboo was often not more than a few feet. There is a
true story of an officer who, during the later stages of the
campaign, was working his way round a steep hillside with
his platoon and suddenly heard the sound of angry voices
apparently coming from directly below his feet. A cautious
investigation revealed that he was standing on top of a
Japanese bunker, whose occupants were protesting against
the showers of earth caused by his thoughtless activity
above.

Early in December 1944 the Allied offensive began, and
on the 15th the 82nd West Africans took Buthidaung,
opening the road from Maungdaw to the Kalapanzin
River. Meanwhile, the 81st West Africans, advancing down
the Kaldan Valley, attacked the Japanese communications
centre at Myohaung; the town fell on January 25 to a
pincer movement by the 81st Division from the north and
the 82nd from the west.

With the opening of the road from Maungdaw, Christison
was able to ship a queer selection of river craft (which he
had previously collected around Maungdaw) over the
Mayu Range to the Kalapanzin River. Supported by these,
the 25th Indian Division advanced on Foul Point at the tip
of the Mayu Peninsula, from which they occupied Kadaung

"A COG IN THE WAR MACHINE"—*a Salisbury artist's tribute
to the R.A.R. published in the* Rhodesia Herald, *28th March,
1941.*

In East Africa, F. E. Harris (Minister of Defence) visited the R.A.R. and is seen inspecting the African Warrant Officers. Lieutenant-Colonel Goode, the Commanding Officer, stands nearest the camera on the left.

A wary askari of the East African Division stands guard in Burma in 1944.

Askaris of the East African Division patrolling a river in a home-made raft, Burma 1944.

Island. Here they prepared for an attack on Akyab, separated from Kadaung Island by a narrow channel. On January 2, however, a young artillery officer flying over the island in a light plane, noticed that the inhabitants were waving to him in what appeared to be a friendly way. Taking a chance he landed on the Akyab airstrip—and found that he had captured the island single-handed. Unknown to Intelligence the last Japanese soldier had pulled out only forty-eight hours earlier.

The enemy were now vulnerable, for in accord with Kimura's orders they were in the process of withdrawing to the east. The only possible line of withdrawal for their guns and vehicles, however, lay along the coastal road running from Kyauktaw to the An and Taungup Passes. If the road ahead of them were cut they would be trapped, and this is precisely what Christison now set about doing.

On January 12 a commando brigade landed on the Myebon Peninsula, thirty miles east of Akyab, quickly followed in support by a brigade of the 25th Division. The enemy was caught unprepared, but quickly collecting his forces he launched a fierce counter-attack. This was repulsed, however, and the arduous task of clearing the whole peninsula then began. On January 22 a second landing was made at Kangaw. This time the commandos met strong resistance from an enemy who had suddenly realised the real threat behind these seemingly isolated attacks. The following night a brigade of the 25th Division was landed in support, and the enemy driven off. On January 29 Kangaw was taken. A road-block was established south of the village, and the Japanese escape route was effectually closed. Troops pushing east from the bridgehead on the Myebon Peninsula linked up with the van of the 82nd West Africans advancing from the north on to Kangaw. The Japanese, caught in the closing jaws of this massive vice, scattered into the hills, leaving behind over a thousand dead, and enormous quantities of vehicles, guns and equipment.

The Rhodesian African Rifles, meanwhile, arrived at Chittagong on December 10, 1944, coming under command of the 82nd West Africans, and given the subsidiary task of guarding the 25th Indian Division's lines of communication. By mid-December the Regiment was making its way along the road to Razabil, and spent Christmas Day at Ngong, eating a dinner of M and V rations and biscuits. Christmas parcels from home were destined to catch up with the men only much later. (It is worth noting that during their service in Burma the Rhodesians received many "comforts" and parcels from appreciative charitable organisations at home. Always welcome, the parcels nevertheless sometimes contained surprises for the unwary. African women's organisations, for example, had been persuaded to knit socks for the askari. Some of the more enthusiastic younger ladies took to writing little notes, containing their names and addresses, and secreting them in the finished articles. The practice came to light when an epidemic of blistered feet swept the Battalion; the jungle warriors, unused to such courtesies, had put on their socks without discovering the notes.) On Boxing Day morale was given a boost by the announcement that the 22nd East Africans would have their own distinctive shoulder-flash—a white elephant.

The Regiment spent New Year's Day, 1945, in the area of Tunnels Pass, midway between Maungdaw and Buthidaung, which had been cleared two weeks earlier by the 82nd Division. For the next three weeks it patrolled the area while Akyab, the Myebon Peninsula, and Kangaw were taken. Sergeant Mbunyunu (837) of "B" Company has left us an entertaining account of one of these patrols:

'I left our camp with five men from the platoon very early one Sunday morning, just after dawn. Before starting we had hot coffee, biscuits and rice. Our uniform was a fairly light green in colour and all the brasses on our kit had been blackened over. We carried our big packs on our backs with food, blankets and medicines inside them. We also carried mosquito nets and capes—known as "gas capes". These capes are used if the enemy should make poisoned air come into your path. I cannot explain what gas is. It is something which you cannot see and do not want to smell.

I had a good map of the country so it was not hard to find the way. I did not even need to use my compass. The map was so good it showed small paths over the mountains. On leaving camp we walked along a path through the hills until we reached a river. Then we left the path and walked up the river bed. The banks of the river were so high, and the bamboo grew so thickly on them, that the bamboos on each bank met over our heads and the sun was not able to lighten our walk. The journey was dark and wet. After some time we were able to leave the river and take to a small path up a steep hill, many hundreds of feet high. Then the path finished and we had to cut our own way through the forest and bamboos, using our great knives [pangas]. It took us three hours to cut our way to the top of even a small hill. When we reached our journey's end we found the enemy had gone.

The enemy had dug good trenches, and made good places for fighting, but they ran off before we got there leaving lots of clothing and other kit behind them. We had to be very careful where we walked because the enemy had made all sorts of traps to catch us. They used grenades to explode under our feet, and in some places they laid mines to destroy us. In one place we found the dead body of an enemy soldier. His kit was near him, and his helmet still shaded his face. We thought at first that he was alive, and prepared to attack him.

By the time we had finished looking over the position it was late afternoon, so we moved on, and then prepared dinner. We camped for the night, after tucking our nets about us so the mosquitoes could not annoy us. Next morning we set off again and, travelling slowly, reached a place where there had been much fighting. We saw damaged guns, wagons, tanks and so on. We saw where soldiers of the enemy had been buried. Passing on we came to bridges over other streams, but they had all been destroyed by the enemy who had run off.

Now we thought it was time to return to the Regiment, and on our way back we were wise to travel carefully. In one place some mines had been put in the path, but—fortunately for us—the enemy had not quite hidden the traps below the earth and our men, having sharp eyes, saw the danger in good time. We reached the Regiment at noon the next day, having learnt much of interest.'

For many of the 22nd East African Brigade this was their first experience of the risks and dangers of an active front. To the Rhodesian African Rifles it represented the fruition of years of training, and an opportunity to prove that the persevering faith and doggedness of men who had struggled to keep the Regiment alive during those years had not been wasted.

On January 21 the 26th Indian Division landed on Ramree Island and seized Kyaukpyu at its northern tip. The enemy scattered, and in a number of small groups dispersed into secret corners of the island. Ramree is, at its widest, some twenty miles broad and fifty miles long and hunting the Japanese in its thick jungle and swamp was a difficult and dangerous task. The East Africans were called forward to help in the mopping-up operations. Early in February they moved down the Mayu Range by road to Foul Point where they boarded landing-craft and swung across the five-mile wide channel to Akyab. The move was completed by February 4, and after a short stay they again set sail, this time in a Henderson liner, for Ramree, which they reached on February 19. By the 21st they were well dug in at Minbyin, Kyaukale and Mayin, and had assumed responsibility for the defence of the Kaukpyu area and for patrolling south of it.

Between February 18 and 20, the Brigade was visited by the G.O.C., East Africa Command. His visit was enlivened by a Japanese aircraft which, making its approach to bomb Kyaukpyu airstrip, flew a mere 500 feet over the mess where he was dining. It was one of the last times the

Map B

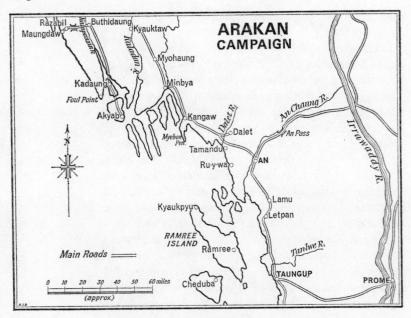

Brigade sighted enemy aircraft, for subsequently, on the mainland, they rarely flew near.

About this time General Sir Oliver Leese ordered Christison to:

(i) develop Akyab and Ramree as air-supply bases for the Fourteenth Army.

(ii) clear north and central Arakan.

(iii) seize a bridgehead at Taungup, fifty miles south of Akyab.

(iv) open the Taungup—Prome Road, if possible before the approaching monsoon.

The Japanese had been badly shaken and had suffered severe losses. The survivors of their 54th Division were now protecting the passes at An and Taungup and, in accordance with their orders, blocking the way east (the

55th Division had already withdrawn to the Prome–Henzada area).

Christison planned to confront the enemy first at An, and on February 4 the 82nd West Africans (less the 22nd Brigade) were ordered up the watercourse of the Dalet Chaung. Their mission was to attack the An Pass from the north-west simultaneous with a brigade of the 26th Division which landed, on February 16, at Ru-y-wa with orders to attack from the south. These operations were well under way when, at the beginning of March, they had to be called off. Because of the difficulties of terrain the encircling columns could be supplied only by air, but with the battle in Central Burma approaching its climax, Slim needed every aircraft he could lay hands on. The needs of the Arakan Campaign yielded to more imperative demands, and General Leese transferred the bulk of the 15th Corps' aircraft to the main front. The advance on An was immediately halted and the West Africans ordered back to the coast. It would not be until May 11 that An—deserted by the enemy—fell into the Allies' hands.

Balked by circumstances beyond his control, Christison nevertheless attempted to complete the remainder of his tasks, concentrating primarily on clearing the Taungup–Prome Road. Although he still retained minimal air support, Christison had to rely for the transport of bulk supplies and of men mainly on his tiny fleet of minesweepers and somewhat decrepit landing-craft. In the first week of March he landed the 4th Indian Brigade at Letpan—thirty-five miles north of Taungup—which immediately pushed south down the narrowing coastal corridor.

The Rhodesian African Rifles, languishing on Ramree, where, according to one askari, they had "made camp on the seashore and after nearly a month of sea-bathing felt very fit and hardy," were ordered to pack away all extraneous kit and be prepared for a move. They had not yet made any real contact with the enemy, but combat lay not far ahead. On March 16 they embarked from Kyaukpyu beach in six minesweepers and H.M. Destroyer *Esquimo*, bound for Ru-y-wa (ninety miles north of Letpan) where a brigade of the 25th Division maintained a bridgehead. On arrival the East Africans came under the command of Major-General H. C. Stockwell. One officer vividly recalls the voyage from Ramree:

'The landing of the 22nd Brigade on the beachhead at Ru-y-wa was carried out by the Navy. We embarked on minesweepers, 150 troops to each ship. On my own ship there was good food and drink to be had in the tiny wardroom and time passed pleasantly enough; but I did look out occasionally to see how the troops were doing. One stolid African I saw, who had hopefully joined together eight pullthroughs, was happily fishing over the stern. I did not trouble to tell him that the whole fleet, with destroyer escort, was crashing along at eighteen knots. On the same minesweeper the Chief Petty Officer thought it a good imperial gesture to consolidate the entire crews' rum ration for the day and present it to our senior African sergeant. Fortunately this noble generosity was spotted in time and diplomatic settlement achieved. I forget how it went, but we kept the gift in trust for him.'

On March 18 the Brigade received orders to proceed south from Ru-y-wa, along the coast past Letpan, and join the 4th Indian Brigade which was engaging the enemy at Taungup. The journey was to be made with all possible speed, ten days being the maximum limit. Difficulties needed no seeking. Although the main Japanese concentration was still at An there were considerable enemy forces operating in the jungle-clad hills south of Ru-y-wa, and the natural obstacles included several hazardous *chaung* crossings and, of course, the thick tangles of bamboo. Moreover, the war-worn transport bequeathed to the Brigade by the 82nd West Africans was in a pitiable state. Despite much effort on the part of the mechanics only sixteen trucks were eventually pronounced serviceable and it was decided that the vehicles would be used solely to ferry food and ammunition.

The enemy was anxious to retain command of the Taungup–Prome Road, especially until the approaching monsoon was well into season, thus delaying British pursuit in the lower reaches of the Irrawaddy. But the broken remnants of the Japanese divisions were in a pitiable condition. Lack of wholesome food and of medical supplies had resulted in local outbreaks of cholera, widespread *beri-beri*, and an almost total incidence of malaria. The soldiers of the Emperor, arrogantly confident not very many months before, were at long last on the run.

Chapter
5
Tanlwe Chaung

DAY after day, contact with the enemy drew closer. Patrols regularly began to find signs of Japanese and an ammunition dump was blown up at Yo Chaung. Night-time "jitter-parties" sparked by marauding Japanese became commonplace.

On March 25, the 22nd Brigade, with the King's African Rifles in the lead and the Rhodesian African Rifles in the rear to assist in ferrying stores, reached and seized the high ground overlooking the Kwegu Crossing on the An Chaung. During that afternoon three landing-craft arrived from Tamandu with supplies—also on board were a number of Indian labourers. Two companies of the K.A.R. had, meanwhile, swum across the chaung, and the remainder, together with the Northern Rhodesia Regiment, had been ferried across. They were accompanied by "A" Company and a platoon of "D" Company, Rhodesian African Rifles, who had been detailed to help with the unloading of the stores. Thinking that the area (having been traversed by two battalions) was secure, "A" Company worked far into the night, leaving protective duties to the platoon from "D" Company. The platoon stationed itself on top a small rise near the off-loading area which had recently been used by the enemy as a defensive position. When a halt was finally called to the labour, a tired "A" Company without bothering to dig slit-trenches put down their mosquito nets and slept in disordered confusion among the Indians. An askari from "D" Company recounts what followed:

'Now I want to tell you of the first Jap soldier we killed. We had just crossed over a large river, and were working

4

late in the day to get our food and other stores unloaded. One company was left near the river bank to guard the stores, whilst a platoon of men were sent to a small hill a few hundred yards from the river.

Very early the next morning the Japanese attacked. The dawn had just broken when we heard quiet voices some distance away. Our sentry called out, inquiring who it was. At once there came a reply in the form of a burst of machine-gun fire. Then we could faintly see the figures in the dim light; they were Japanese soldiers. We had the wisdom of digging slit-trenches proved us then, for had we not had those trenches the Japs would have done us much damage with their machine-guns. However, one of us took a shot at the figures and there was a loud yell showing that one of them had been hit. The enemy then went away.

When it was light we looked for the Japs, but they had gone right away. We saw much blood about, and following that spoor we found that the Japs had dragged the man we had wounded away. Later we found his body in a well, where his comrades had thrown it. He had been shot through the head.

The Japanese do not like fighting in the daytime; they wait until it is dark, and then come round our camp throwing grenades and firing machine-guns.'

The Regiment, still apprentices in the craft of war, was fast learning its trade. This action taught them three sharp lessons—never fail to dig slit-trenches, never assume an area was free of Japanese, and never sleep bunched with the Indian labourers, for they were likely to add to the confusion of battle. Luckily, on this occasion, the Indians had only half a dozen rifles between them and their indiscriminate firing did little damage.

It had been intended to pass the Rhodesians into the lead at Kwegu, but the Corps Commander could not afford the one-day delay the move would have required, and the K.A.R., therefore, was ordered to push on to Letpan with a minimum of equipment and supplies. By the 28th, the crossing of An Chaung had been completed.

Nightfall always brought with it the nerve-shattering unpleasantness of Japanese jitter-parties. Often very effective, they will not easily be forgotten by the men who endured them. One Company Commander noted in his diary:

'28th March: Move 2½ miles to An Chaung. Take over from C Company, 3NRR. We are 4th Group rearguard. Evidence of Japs is to be seen everywhere. 300 have been reported three miles down the road. Two of "D" Company were killed last night.

3rd April: Moved on to Hinywet, and settled in position expecting a quiet night. But what a night it turned out. Our casualties were one killed and nine wounded. We were delayed today, having to send our casualties back through the West Africans. Could not have done without them.'

An askari recalls:

'The Japanese soldiers did not like our being on their heels all the time, and although they would not attack us in the daytime, they frequently worried us at night. In one of the night attacks Private Judzi (2163) had a lucky escape. An enemy soldier threw a grenade at us. It struck Judzi's rifle just as he was firing at a Jap. The bomb exploded, of course, and Judzi was left holding only a tiny piece of his rifle—the rest of it had disappeared in small bits. Judzi received no hurt at all.'

Another officer recalls the efficiency of the jitter-parties.

'At night there was no question of where to go; climb to the top and dig. It needed little tactical training to know that the hilltops could be made safe and cosy with all-round defence. Nobody cared who used the roads and paths at night.

Many of our slit-trenches for a night's occupation were roofed with bamboo and an earth covering. Most comforting of all were the *pangyis* or sharpened bamboo stakes; 3 or 4 foot long, and planted thickly round the company perimeter, or covering a hidden approach. It would take a resourceful or cunning Jap, we thought, to brave an enclosure bristling with *pangyis*.'

We ourselves never moved outside a perimeter after dark, and it was as much as a man's life was worth even to attempt to relieve nature more than a yard from his slit-trench or sleeping hollow. Our fellows were trigger conscious and grenade happy. For a long time the slightest sound, or the croaking of a tree frog, would bring a shower of grenades and a burst of sten. "D" Company gained a name that way, and were known in the Battalion as "D Company Grenadiers".'

This, of course, was exactly the reaction hoped for by the Japanese. Gunflashes enabled the enemy to pinpoint the precise location of the firer. It therefore became the practice to fine anyone who fired his weapon without good reason, ten days' stoppage of pay.

Between An and Mai Chaungs movement was restricted to definite bounds. The Brigade was accordingly organised into three battalion Groups, and a fourth Group comprised of one company from each battalion. This latter Group was ordered to protect the supply depot established at Kwegu until the failing transport could manage to clear the stores forward. Two of the precious vehicles had already been destroyed by mines planted on the road verges. On March 28 the Regiment moved south—two days behind the King's African Rifles, who reached Sane (eight miles from Letpan) that same day. The Northern Rhodesians moved on March 29, and the advance continued at that interval to Hinywet, Talaindaugn, Sane and Letpan. On the 30th the Battalion arrived at Sane, and on the 31st crossed the Mai Chaung. By April 1 the Brigade Group, less the Kwegu garrison, had firmly established itself south of the chaung. A new depot was sited, and the Kwegu troops were ordered to follow up and hold the Mai Chaung ferry until relieved by the 2nd West African Brigade following close behind. The first half of the Brigade mission was completed; the East Africans had done well in crossing some forty miles of dense, enemy-infested jungle in a little over four days.

After a day at Letpan, the Brigade was ordered to march as rapidly as possible to the area of Dalaba Village, on the Tanlwe Chaung. The Rhodesian African Rifles—less "C" Company (seconded to the Kwegu garrison) and "A" Company (left at Letpan to protect supplies)—were ordered to march twelve miles to Lamu. From here they would be carried the remaining twenty-two miles to Dalaba in transport supplied by the 26th Division. Setting out before first-light, the men arrived at Lamu just before 8.00 a.m., only to find that the transport could take no more than two companies. Headquarters Company, therefore, set off to march the rest of the way, rejoining the Battalion at Kindaunggyi two days later.

To the south-west the 4th Indian Brigade had been advancing on Taungup and, by April 2, had secured the high ground overlooking the village. The 26th Indian Division to which they belonged, however, was now withdrawn to prepare for the attack on Rangoon, and the 82nd West Africans took over their operations. On April 3 the East Africans received orders to operate against the northern flank of the Japanese holding the Taungup area. The 2nd West African Brigade was to occupy Taungup, and having done so to drive eastwards across the Taungup Chaung. At the same time, the 22nd East African Brigade was to execute a wide encircling move along the course of the Tanlwe Chaung and at a convenient point, leave the river and break south across the jungle, meeting the West Africans on the Taungup–Prome Road, about ten miles from the town. In anticipation of this advance the K.A.R. patrolled east up the Tanlwe Chaung from a firm base at Kyibin, and the N.R.R. patrolled in the general direction of the Yebok Chaung. The Regiment was occupied in affording close protection to Divisional Headquarters, and was rejoined on April 5 and 7 by "A" and "C" Companies.

Patrols of the K.A.R. had located units of the Japanese 121st Regiment in the Yapale area, and it was now decided to move the Brigade to Palawa, taking Yapale on the way. Leaving "D" Company to protect Brigade Headquarters, the Regiment moved to Kyibin, where "A" Company was detached to Wundun to provide a guard for the guns of the Gold Coast artillery, and also for Engineers bulldozing a road forward. "B" Company patrols in the area were ordered to locate an enemy patrol which had been recently engaged against the Northern Rhodesians with some success. The patrol was never found, but "B" Company did retrieve, and bury, the bodies of an officer and three askari who had been killed in the engagement. A new hazard was added to the normal dangers of patrolling by the swollen, and rapid flowing, waters of the chaung. Often boats had to be used to ferry the troops (a profitable occupation for the Burmese boatmen) and one askari drowned during this period.

On April 9 the attack against Yapale was initiated with an airstrike by seventeen Spitfires. Three days later a further strike was made by forty-seven aircraft followed by a successful assault involving the K.A.R. and the N.R.R., supported by artillery. The use of aircraft in this action had an unfortunate sequel for the Regiment because it attracted elements of the Japanese Air Force to the area, and an attempt to evacuate three African casualties by air on the 13th met with disaster when the aircraft was shot down, and all aboard it killed.

On April 16 the Regiment took the lead, and advanced to Taikywa, where they received information from their forward unit—"D" Company—that the enemy had been seen in the village of Dalet, some two miles ahead. Late in the evening the Company had spotted a number of Japanese moving about—apparently chasing chickens. The Regiment took up positions, preparatory to attacking the following morning, but at dawn found that the enemy had disappeared. Much to their disgust, a patrol working behind them, acting on a report from a party of signallers, had had a vigorous encounter with the enemy at Taikywa and had driven them into the bamboo. Assuming that the Japanese were still in the vicinity, artillery and mortar fire was directed on to a suspicious-looking hill, *Cross*, south of the village. A platoon was also sent across to make a thorough search of the area. It reported that both Dalet and the lower slopes of the hill appeared clear, and "D" Company began to cross the *chaung*.

Suddenly, when they were in the middle of the river and well out in the open, they came under a hail of machine-gun fire from a point farther down the *chaung*. Wavering for only a moment, they pressed forward and up the hill. Here they found positions only lately vacated by the enemy and, judging by the amount of kit strewn about, vacated in a hurry. Meanwhile, a platoon under Lieutenant Ross Walker was sent to investigate the area from which the firing had come. Struggling through some very difficult country, the platoon came upon the rear of the enemy position, about 800 yards south of *Cross* where they found a small party of Japanese, armed with machine-guns and cup-dischargers for grenades. The light was failing rapidly and Walker decided to secure the patrol for the night on a small hump close by and in the event of not being discovered attack in the early hours of the morning. As they moved stealthily away, however, there was a burst of fire and Walker, calling out to his leading scout, received no reply. On calling to the second scout he heard him shout back that he was wounded, caught by his pack in the bamboo, and unable to move. Ordering his Bren-gunner to lay down covering fire, Lieutenant Walker went to the rescue. While he was trying to disentangle the wounded man a second burst of fire killed the scout and wounded Walker through the shoulder. Leaving the body, he crawled back to the platoon to find that four more askari had been wounded, and were being attended by the medical orderly, Private Mirimi, who seemed quite unconscious of the bullets whipping around him. Realising that he could do no more, Walker withdrew the platoon and, despite his own wound, the drag of four wounded askari, and the nearly impenetrable country through which they had to struggle, returned to *Cross* by 9.00 a.m. the following morning. For their gallant actions Walker was Mentioned in Dispatches, and Mirimi was awarded a Certificate of Gallantry. That night the enemy rearguard withdrew south-eastwards up the *chaung*.

On April 18 supplies ferried by air began to reach the 22nd Brigade for the first time. In general, the system worked very satisfactorily, and the Dakotas did magnificent work. Despite difficult approach runs, often in the face of artillery and mortar fire (and even, on occasion, small-arms fire) no aircraft was ever shot down and, so far as is known, only two crewmen were injured.

The Brigade had now reached the planned change of course in its advance and struck due south across three miles of dense jungle to gain the Taungup Chaung. From here a final advance of just over two miles would be needed to reach the Taungup–Prome Road—the ultimate destination. Patrols indicated that the enemy were holding the ground between the two chaungs in force, and in country ideally suited to defence. A medley of razor-edged ridges covered in dense bamboo, and isolated hills with precipitous slopes now faced the East Africans. The Japanese had sited their defence in depth, extending westwards and covering a number of tough-looking hills code-named *Lamour*, *Valerie*, *Bergner*, *Shearer*, *Lockwood* and *Landis*. The original plan had been to surprise the Japanese with a long, flanking march, but this was abandoned after closer observation showed that the terrain made this if not impossible, at least impracticable. Instead, it was decided to secure the commanding heights of *Bergner* and *Valerie* by frontal assault, and having done so, to exploit the area southwards. The assault upon these two features was entrusted to the Rhodesians.

Map C

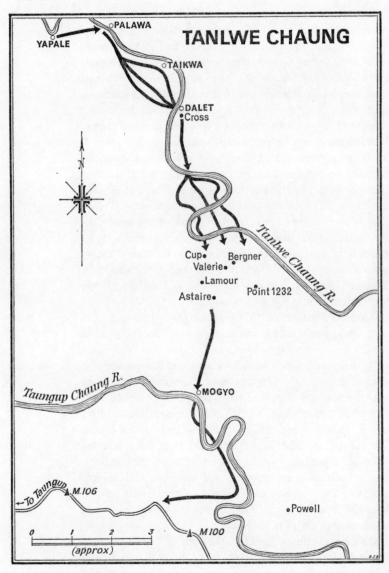

YAPALE
PALAWA
TANLWE CHAUNG
TAIKWA
DALET
Cross
N
Cup
Bergner
Valerie
Tanlwe Chaung R.
Lamour
Astaire
Point 1232
Taungup Chaung R.
MOGYO
To Taungup
M.106
Powell
0 1 2 3
(approx)
M.100

With the object of pinpointing the enemy positions, deep patrolling by "C" and "D" Companies began on April 23. "D" Company concentrated on *Bergner*, and "C" Company on *Valerie*. April 24 was spent in similar fashion. The last patrol of that day—from "D" Company—moving south-east from the river, confirmed that there were two light machine-guns firing straight down the track, another on the eastern slopes of *Bergner*, and a medium machine-gun (its precise location could not be pinpointed) enfilading the approach to *Bergner* from the north-eastern edges of *Valerie*. In addition to locating these positions, the patrol also noted that the askari had begun to assign some sort of hoodoo to *Bergner* and, on approaching it, were showing evident sign of nervousness. In a frontal assault of the type contemplated it is essential that forward momentum be maintained, and it was decided that, if the necessary "dash" was to be sustained, the attack would have to be staged by another Company. The cost of gaining all this information was one officer and one askari wounded.

The final plan was that "A" Company, passing through "D" Company, would attack and take *Bergner*. Its 3rd platoon would then swing right and assault *Valerie*, with "D" Company following close behind to assist in occupation and consolidation. "D" Company was then to exploit the track which ran south from *Valerie*. The attack would be supported by a preliminary airstrike on *Bergner*, followed by a heavy artillery concentration on both hills provided by the West Africans. The Regiment's own three-inch mortars were to superimpose their fire on that of the artillery, paying particular attention to the southern and reverse slopes of *Bergner*, and the K.A.R.'s mortars were also to join the bombardment, concentrating their fire on the north-eastern slopes of *Valerie*.

On the morning of the 26th, the men of "D" Company lay in position some 400 yards from the enemy trenches. "A" Company, ready to pass through together with the mortars, were just behind them, and some 2,000 yards in the rear the West African howitzers were being trained on *Bergner*.

At 0905 hours the Hurricane bombers flew overhead, and were directed on to their targets on *Bergner* by smoke bombs fired by mortars. The hill was strafed, and the bombers released their loads, setting the bamboo on fire and shaking *Valerie* with near-misses. "A" Company started to wriggle forward until they were about 200 yards from the Japanese positions. The noise was intense, and grew still louder as the artillery and mortars began to add their contribution to the barrage. Under cover of the bombardment, the men of "A" Company crawled closer. As the leading platoon reached a point some 100 yards from the enemy, the artillery switched their fire to *Valerie*, strengthening the K.A.R. mortar fire, which had not been effective. This was the signal for the men of "A" Company to charge up the slope, yelling their war cry: "Ngadhla—DHZI! Mamo! Ngadhla—DHZI!"

2 platoon, in the lead, arrived at the top of the hill to find that they had caught the enemy in the open. During the air and artillery bombardment the Japanese had left their foxholes and sheltered on the reverse slope. The askari met them on the way back and, shooting from the hip, chased them straight down the slope again. Here the Japanese halted briefly to return a largely inaccurate fire before retiring into the *chaung*.

According to plan, 4 platoon, commanded by Lieutenant Wilkes, now swung right to occupy *Valerie*, while 3 platoon raced forward to help in the consolidation of *Bergner*. At this stage things started to go awry. 4 platoon, on reaching a small hill about fifty yards from *Bergner*, incorrectly assumed that this was *Valerie*, and halted. Not only did they lose precious momentum, but, far worse, gave the Japanese on *Valerie* time to regain theirs. "D" Company's leading platoon now arrived on the rise to join 4 platoon, and they both came under fire from a well-hidden medium machine-gun located some distance away. An appalling discovery was now made. The assault would have to be made along a single narrow track which ran from the rise to the real *Valerie*. Moving into the lead, "D" Company's 13 platoon, with a section from 4 platoon, started along the track. The enemy immediately opened up with the medium machine-gun and several light machine-guns, covering the confined area with an effective and deadly fire. The enemy weapons also had the advantage of being well concealed in the thick bamboo, the light machine-guns being especially difficult to spot as they changed positions frequently. Struggling and fighting their way up the track, 13 platoon encountered another difficulty. A large tree had been felled straight down the path with its branches pointing towards the attackers. Covered by short-range machine-gun fire, and with impenetrable jungle on either side it presented a serious obstacle. As they reached it the platoon commander was wounded by a treetop sniper (who was himself killed a moment later). Leaderless and pinned down, the askari began to suffer heavy casualties. The Company Commander —Major Stan Morris—realising what had happened, immediately went forward and took command. Following him round the tree, the troops recovered their morale and charged. After a short, sharp struggle, they drove the enemy off *Valerie* and set about consolidating their victory.

The Battalion sustained heavy casualties that morning. Seven askari were killed, and one officer and twenty-two askari wounded, the majority from "D" Company. Of the enemy, six were killed outright (one of whom had been the medium machine-gunner), but although others had been seen to drop over the steep sides of the hill no other definite enemy casualties could be established. A large quantity of equipment and weapons was captured, however, including a Japanese flag, and that evening a signal was received at

Brigade Headquarters from the Divisional Commander
which read:

'A fine action by your R.A.R. and N.R.R. Please convey
my congratulations to all ranks on their splendid fighting
spirit. Your battle is being followed with the closest
interest, and the result will bring a real victory in the
battle of Taungup.'

But the day's work was far from ended. By nightfall, "A"
Company had dug themselves in on *Bergner*, and "D"
Company on *Valerie*. "C" Company and H.Q. Company had
located themselves on *Cup*, a few hundred yards to the
north-west. Hardly had darkness fallen, when the Japanese
began shelling and mortaring "A" Company who, silhouetted
against the burning bamboo, were in a vulnerable position.
Eventually a direct hit on a slit-trench killed three askari
and wounded a fourth. Later, a particularly vigorous
jitter-party visited the area of *Cup* and caused chaos. Some
of the troops, frightened by the grenades falling inside the
defence perimeter, panicked and tried to get away,
others followed, and soon the flight had become general.
Indiscriminate fire and hurtling grenades came from every
direction. Many of the askari took shelter in a near-by
stream, where they were mistaken for enemy and shot at.
Before order was finally restored, four askari had been
killed and one European non-commissioned officer and
eight askari wounded—the majority of them from bullets
probably fired by their own comrades.

This incident removed a little of the glitter from what
had otherwise been a day of significant moment, for the
Regiment had made its first deliberate "set-piece" attack,
and had successfully accomplished its mission. The anniver-
sary of the battle for *Bergner* and *Valerie* is now commemor-
ated each year as "Tanlwe Chaung Day," when old friends
are invited to visit the Battalion in their barracks, and re-
live a little the events of that decisive day.

Chapter
6
The Last Phase

THE capture of *Valerie* and *Bergner* had made little overall impression on the Japanese defences which stretched before the East Africans, and it was obvious that the Brigade would have to fight for every yard of jungle that lay betweem them and the Taungup–Prome Road. On April 27 aggressive patrolling was resumed, and the advance continued. At the cost of a number of casualties, including a Company Commander and a Company second-in-command from the King's African Rifles, *Landis*, *Hope*, and *Loy* were captured—features which formed the western flank of the enemy's defence, centred on *Astaire*.

While these attacks were being pressed home, a patrol from "B" Company, R.A.R., was sent to investigate the area of the hill designated *Point 1232*. Climbing the slope, the leading scout was surprised to see an enemy soldier apparently emerging from the ground a few yards in front of him. He bayoneted the equally startled Japanese, but immediately another emerged from the bunker, who shot and wounded the scout. Within seconds bullets and grenade shrapnel filled the air, the thick bamboo, which effectively concealed the enemy positions, adding to the growing confusion. The patrol began to withdraw when the section-commander suddenly fell, wounded. His second-in-command under covering-fire from the Bren-gunner crawled forward and dragged his leader to safety. While he was thus engaged, the Bren—with one long burst—managed to silence the enemy medium machine-gun. Then, leaving a rearguard of two men beside the track, the patrol retreated. Hardly had they done so when a Japanese soldier emerged from the bamboo and started down the track. The hidden askari allowed him to approach within fifteen yards, and then shot him dead.

From the information gathered by this patrol it was decided that *Point 1232* was held in at least platoon strength, supported by two light machine-guns and one medium machine-gun (although it was possible that the latter had been destroyed during the patrol engagement). Accordingly, the feature was subjected to a prolonged artillery and mortar bombardment culminating, on April 30, with an airstrike. A reconnaisance patrol was then sent to investigate, and found the area clear of Japanese, although there was considerable evidence to show that they had been present during the artillery and air bombardment.

That night the Japanese artillery was exceptionally active, and at dawn the next morning patrols found that under cover of this barrage the enemy had evacuated the entire area. It was estimated that during the week's fighting some sixty Japanese had been killed and as many wounded, but as usual few bodies were found.

The Brigade now began its advance on Mogyo, with the King's African Rifles in the lead. Their orders were to seize the village and establish a dropping-zone nearby. The operation was completed without incident, and on May 1 the Brigade reached the Taungup Chaung.

The enemy, meanwhile, had re-grouped for his final stand. The pivot of his defence was the hill *Powell*. From here he commanded clear all-round fields of fire and the position was well supported in rear by a variety of guns and mortars sighted in depth on the Taungup–Prome Road. An added advantage was an unobstructed view of the Taungup Chaung, running from north to south in front of *Powell*.

On May 2, with "D" Company R.A.R. leading, the Brigade started south, following the course of the *chaung*.

After steady progress they reached an ox-bow bend in the river, and started to cross. At this point "D" Company was discovered and the enemy on *Powell* immediately opened fire with machine-guns. The range, fortunately, was too great for the fire to be properly effective, and the company managed to secure themselves on the south bank of the river with the loss of only two wounded. The advance ground to a temporary halt.

And then, with their goal so near, the Brigade's hopes of a quick victory were smashed by the arrival of the pelting monsoon rains. Following close behind the East Africans, the Engineers—ignoring the distractions of enemy and terrain—had been constructing a jeep-track. Now this steep, earthen road quickly turned into a slimy, impassable, morass and all hope of bringing guns or vehicles forward was dashed. At this crucial moment, therefore, the Brigade was faced, not only with the rapidly deteriorating weather but, more importantly, with a total lack of artillery support.

On May 4 it was learned that elements of the Gold Coast Regiment had reached *Milestone 100* on the Taungup–Prome Road, and the Regiment was ordered to press forward and complete the link-up by the next day. *Powell*, however, still barred the way. Despite the urgency involved, the lack of artillery cover necessitated that the Regiment proceed cautiously in dealing with what was obviously going to be a very tough proposition. A patrol from "B" Company was therefore sent to reconnoitre the area. Understandably in that terrain the patrol lost its way and investigated a quite different feature, which they reported to be clear of enemy. At the same time, a patrol from "A" Company, after a short engagement with an enemy patrol in a small village north of *Powell*, came across a Japanese supply dump showing evident signs of recent evacuation. On the strength of these two reports it was assumed that the Japanese had withdrawn from the area. In the early hours of May 5, "B" Company, closely followed by "C" Company, moved up the slope of *Powell*. Near the top, they emerged from the jungle and found themselves facing the crest which, though itself thickly covered by bamboo, was surrounded on three sides by a wide expanse of open ground. The two leading platoons of "B" Company started to cross, and had almost reached the jungle on the far side when pandemonium broke loose. They had walked into a trap. A vicious cross-fire from mortars, rifles, machine-guns, and a seventy-millimetre gun was opened up from their immediate front and both flanks. In the first few seconds four askari were killed and six wounded (one of whom died later) and an "over" from the seventy-millimetre gun landed amongst the leading section of "C" Company, killing one askari and wounding another.

The leading platoon began a hasty retreat, and the other tried to manoeuvre into position to provide covering fire. At that moment Sergeant Phillip Moyo (248), picked up a Bren-gun, rushed forward and emptied the magazine into the bamboo, which temporarily halted the enemy fire. Taking advantage of this respite both platoons withdrew hurriedly over the open ground taking with them, as they thought, their wounded. But when they regained the cover of the bamboo they heard shouting from the direction of the Japanese position and, looking back, saw the "C" Company Sergeant-major, W.O.II Elijah (157), crawling from body to body, seemingly indifferent to the bullets whistling over his head. Realising that in the general panic one of the wounded men had been forgotten, Elijah had returned to look for him. Eventually he reached the man, who died at that moment. Quickly a smoke-screen was laid down, and the C.S.M. dashed to safety under its protective fog.

C.S.M. Elijah (who was destined to become Regimental Sergeant-Major) was Mentioned in Despatches for his brave conduct, and Sergeant Moyo received a Certificate of Gallantry.

A new plan of attack now had to be devised against *Powell*, and it was decided to lay down a heavy and lengthy mortar bombardment, followed by an airstrike. The Brigade mortars began ranging in on the hill during the afternoon of May 6, preparatory to the bombardment scheduled for the next morning. Meanwhile, a patrol from "A" Company, followed soon after by the remainder of that company, had skirted the enemy's defences and finally reached the Taungup–Prome Road where they made contact with a patrol from the Gold Coast Regiment.

During the evening patrols reported that the Japanese appeared to be vacating *Powell*. Nevertheless the Battalion was ordered to continue the attack as arranged, and early on the 7th the airstrike was initiated, backed by the Brigade mortars. The Japanese artillery replied, heavily at first, but gradually slackening in tempo. As the enemy fire decreased, a patrol from "B" Company was sent to assess the damage and found that the enemy, in a now familiar tactic, had left their trenches during the bombardment, and were engaged in re-occupying them. Within a very short time the enemy had sufficiently recovered to lay down a heavy mortar and artillery concentration, and once again the attack had to be abandoned. That evening the Brigade was ordered to bypass *Powell* and slip through the hills to the west. The mortars fired one final salvo on to *Powell* before they, together with "B" Company, rejoined the Battalion for the march to the road. The units reached *Milestone 106* a few hours later, and the Northern Rhodesians passed into the lead with orders to press the retreating enemy. Though they travelled almost fifty miles up the road to Prome, however, they never regained contact. The Japanese had fled.

Its task completed, the Brigade was now ordered to build itself protective quarters against the increasingly heavy monsoon rains. Since their arrival in Burma the East Africans had learned much in the art of jungle warfare, but they had paid a high price for their knowledge. In the mud and slime that was the Taungup–Prome Road, they totted up their casualties:

22nd East African Brigade	Killed or died of wounds	Wounded
European Officers and Other Ranks	3	7
African Other Ranks	56	141

The Rhodesian African Rifles

European Officers and Other Ranks	—	5
African Other Ranks	32	67

In a report written after the Campaign, Major W. Walker said:

'The conduct of the askari, most of whom had never experienced enemy fire before, deserves a lasting tribute. Their energy and endurance on the march and on patrol through some of the worst country in the Arakan, their constancy and discipline under the stress of persistent mortar and artillery fire, and their cheerfulness throughout the appalling weather conditions which developed in the latter stages of the operation, were beyond praise.'

That the enemy also respected the askari is evident from the following extract taken from a captured Japanese officer's diary:

'The enemy soldiers are not from Britain, but are from Africa. Because of their beliefs they are not afraid to die, so, even if their comrades have fallen, they keep on advancing as if nothing had happened. They have excellent physique and are very brave, so fighting against these soldiers is somewhat troublesome.'

During the remainder of May the Battalion occupied itself with building quarters, and making themselves as comfortable as possible in surroundings made unpleasant by mud, dripping vegetation and incessant rain. Every soldier is a scavenger, and the askari were no exceptions.

On June 6, Battalion Orders reported that: "Complaints have been received from the village of Hmaman to the effect that thefts of roofing materials have taken place," and ordered that the practice should cease immediately.

In Central Burma the Japanese were retreating south in considerable disorder. From the Irrawaddy Valley to the Sittang River the area was filled with parties of Japanese seeking to rejoin the Japanese 28th Army, now regrouping near Sittang in preparation for an attempted breakout in July. The 22nd Brigade was ordered to assist in stopping the boltholes. Although the Battalion's baggage had only just reached them, it was immediately re-packed and returned to Ramree. On June 21 they set off for Letpadan where they were to come under command of the 20th Indian Division. The Rhodesians started the trip in transport, but had not travelled much more than thirty miles when the road gave out. It had been badly damaged by the R.A.F. during its occupation by the Japanese, and the heavy rains had not improved its surface. It was pronounced unsafe for vehicles, and once more the Regiment had to march. On foot, the Battalion continued the remaining seventy miles to the Irrawaddy, where they were ferried across, finally reaching Prome on June 29. Order and counter-order was received before they were eventually directed to the village of Gyobingauk, some 120 miles north of Rangoon and on the fringe of hilly country known as the Pegu Yomas.

The Brigade was deployed on a wide front and given the task of patrolling the foothills along the western stretches of the Yomas, in order to drive Japanese units in the area across the range and into the eager hands of the Fourteenth Army. The terrain over which they worked was, in parts, so flat that it became flooded at the least hint of rain. In addition, all the well-known (and well-hated) characteristics of Arakan geography and vegetation were present. Because every piece of information had to be evaluated,

long-ranging patrols were often sent out in the dismal
jungle, even though the information volunteered by local
inhabitants was scanty, ill-informed and sometimes
deliberately false. Immense help was given by a local Roman
Catholic missionary, Father Moran, who seemed to exercise
a measure of control over the villagers, and who gave
invaluable aid in assessing the veracity of their reports.

On the whole, the relationship established between the
African soldier and the local Burmese villager was friendly
and hospitable, but at first the askari were puzzled to find
that whenever they entered a Burmese village the inhabitants would run screaming for their lives into the thick
bush. It was only later that they learned the Burmese had
been told by the Japanese that all Africans were cannibals,
and were especially fond of eating the flesh of women and
children. Nor was this story part of a propaganda programme. The Japanese themselves firmly believed it, and
honestly thought that their dead were used to supplement
the meat ration of African regiments.

On arrival at Gyobingauk, "B" and "D" Companies were
united under the command of Major Morris. Designated
Stanforce, they were based at Waing with units stationed
at Yeda and Uyingyi. *Stanforce*—whose supply transport
consisted of bullock carts—had its first encounter with the
enemy on July 6. After a short engagement the patrol
withdrew to report to its Company Commander, who
promptly took it out again to gather more information.
Private Mazonde (2417) takes up the story:

> 'One day on patrol in very thick jungle we saw the dead
> body of a Gurkha soldier lying in front of us, and standing
> against a tree was a clean rifle. We watched carefully, and
> then saw a Jap soldier a short distance away. He could not
> get to his rifle, but unfortunately he turned suddenly
> and saw us. Away he went. In that dense jungle one step
> is enough to take you out of sight of anyone.
>
> Well, we thought we would try to track that Jap, so
> crawling quietly forward we followed his spoor, until at

last we suddenly came upon a Jap position. The Japs
saw one of us and fired. We ducked out of sight and went
back to report our discovery.

Our Company Commander led us off the next morning,
and we were taken to where the Japanese were in their
trenches. As we crept nearer to them the Japs fired at us
and, lying down, we returned their fire. From early
morning until amost noon we shot at them, and all our
nervousness had quite disappeared. We saw that we had
killed several of the Japs, when suddenly they ran off into
the jungle. We advanced into their position, where we
found that they had left much property in their hurry to
get away.'

Six askari were wounded in this action—two of them by a
bomb from the patrol's own mortar, which rebounded off
the bamboo and fell in front of the mortar crew.

On July 8 there was an engagement against a Japanese
defensive position occupied by about sixteen riflemen and
two machine-gunners. As the attackers moved forward,
however, the enemy slipped back, melting away into the
thick bush. Apart from recovering the bodies of two
Gurkhas—which they buried—the Battalion had no
success on this encounter. In fact only one Japanese
soldier was captured throughout this period. He, poor
devil, seemed more frightened of being eaten by the askari
than of anything else. Emaciated by hunger, malnutrition
and disease, he was typical of the Japanese soldiers now
swarming through the jungle towards Sittang. But if the
enemy was on the run, he was not yet defeated, and it is
perhaps indicative of his morale that whenever an empty
Japanese camp was located there was certain to be a sheaf of
surrender-leaflets (many thousands of which were dropped
by the R.A.F. over the jungle) hanging from a nail in the
lavatory.

As the enemy were driven farther and farther into
the hills, life for the R.A.R. became more and more
tedious, with only rare engagements to liven the pace.

Various Japanese base-camps were found—one of which was large enough to house a brigade—and were destroyed. Some patrols took to the water, and navigated the rivers and streams in a variety of ancient and makeshift craft. It was during this period that gangs of dacoits (bandits) began to make their appearance, and occasional encounters with these helped to relieve the increasing boredom. For his energy and leadership during this period, Major Morris was Mentioned in Despatches.

Finally, at the beginning of August, the Brigade started to withdraw from the area and concentrate on Toungoo, where they were to relieve the 62nd Indian Brigade. But before this could be effected a wireless message was received on August 15 confirming the Japanese surrender. The war, at long last, was over. Fighting in the jungle, however, was to continue for some weeks, and the Brigade was kept busy routing out small pockets of Japanese who, lacking wireless communication, remained in ignorance of their Government's capitulation. On September 12, 1945, the formal unconditional surrender of all Japanese forces in South-East Asia was made to Admiral Mountbatten in Singapore.

The process of demobilisation was a slow one, and the Brigade was among the last to leave. During this period it was employed on a number of tasks, principally the repair of a 100-mile stretch of the Mawchi Road. Then, in March 1946, having spent the preceding months in labour-force duties and guarding P.O.W.s, the Brigade moved to Elephant Camp, just outside Rangoon.

The Battalion set sail for Mombasa, via Ceylon, in April, and arrived in Salisbury on May 10. The next day, having repaired as far as they were able the stains of travel, they paraded through the City to the official welcome. The Rhodesian African Rifles had come home.

Epilogue

S OLDIERS, newly returned from the Front, must expect a certain number of eulogies from a proud citizenry. But the eulogies that soldiers most treasure are those delivered by their fellow soldiers; the men who shared with them the jungle, the heat, the discomfort and fear, and above all the agonising tedium.

Shortly after his return to Rhodesia, Captain M. G. Mills wrote:

> 'But for a job well done our Signal Platoon deserved our thanks. They were often incredibly stupid, and got the fair share of blame and curses that usually fall to Signals. Yet never, that I can recall, did a failure to get through hold up a patrol or an action when communication was essential. To carry a 48 wireless set, plus ordinary equipment and food, is a job for a mule, not a man. Signals have to dig, too, for the night, or else be left unpleasantly naked on ground level. They must often patrol in bad country, and meet the ordinary hazards. In one awkward business I have a mental picture of two harassed signallers carefully selecting a large fallen tree trunk to hide behind, and while one crouched low adjusting his wavelength to contact Battalion Headquarters, the other stood erect, and hopefully discharged his rifle in all directions. Honour satisfied, they then proceeded to take down "In" and "Out" messages until the cows came home.'

R.S.M. Stephen Machado, writing in *Muchengeti*, captures something of the spirit of the African soldier.

> 'I am proud to be in this Battalion of brave men who fight, even as do the elephants, in this deep green jungle. We met the enemy, who shelled us violently with his great guns, but they failed to make us turn away from the fight. We fought on until the enemy was outwitted and defeated, and through bravery and the help of God our losses were not big.

Since the birth of the Regiment I have known it.
Since its formation I have done what I could to teach these
men of the Rhodesian African Rifles. I have seen the
glorious results of that teaching of mine and of the
officers of the Regiment.

And today we all smile together. For have we not
fought and risked our lives side by side to keep our land
safe from the horrible things we have seen here ? And the
war being over, we feel that we may think of our fighting
comrades and—having seen what war can cause to people
and to lands—may humbly say *ISHE KOMBORERA
AFRICA*.* We, who have known, sing these words with
our thoughts resting on them, and our eyes seeing
desolate lands, and the graves of the soldiers of the
Rhodesian African Rifles.'

The most lasting tribute of all, however, is found in
Defeat into Victory, written by a great soldier and commander, Field Marshal Viscount Slim:

'The war in Burma was a soldier's war. There comes a
moment in every battle against a stubborn enemy when the
result hangs in the balance. Then the General, however
skilful and far-sighted he may have been, must hand over
to his soldiers, to the men in the ranks and to their
regimental officers, and leave them to complete what he
has begun. The issue then rests with them, on their
courage, their hardihood, their refusal to be beaten either
by the cruel hazards of nature or by the fierce strength of
their human enemy. That moment came early and often
in the fighting in Burma: sometimes it came when
tired, sick men felt alone, when it would have been so
easy for them to give up, when only will, discipline and
faith could steel them to carry on. To the soldiers of
many races who, in the comradeship of the Fourteenth
Army, *did* go on, and to the airmen who flew with them
and fought over them, belongs the true glory of achieve-
ment. It was they who turned Defeat into Victory.'

*God save Africa.

Postscript

I FIRST started collecting material for this book with the intention of covering the Regiment's history from the period of its formation in 1940 until its return from Malaya at the end of 1958. I soon found, however, that I had set myself a mammoth task. No history of the Rhodesian African Rifles had previously been published, and what information there was was both scanty and piecemeal.

Other factors were also involved which made the task difficult, and the circumstance of my departure from Rhodesia (and the source of my references) at the end of 1968 finally decided me to end the book at that point where the Regiment returns from Burma.

The years 1939–1945 saw the birth of the Regiment despite tremendous initial public disapproval; its struggle to establish itself against numerous odds—scarcity of supplies, official indifference, conditions of service which did nothing to help maintain morale—and its emergence as a disciplined fighting unit.

On its return to Salisbury after the War, the Regiment was demobilised, and for a time looked as though it might suffer the same fate as its predecessor, the Rhodesia Native Regiment, and be disbanded. After some intensive lobbying this was prevented, but for a number of years the Regiment existed only in a secondary capacity, more as a labour battalion, only rarely being allowed to fulfil its proper functions.

This undistinguished period came to an end when the Regiment was sent to the Canal Zone, primarily to carry out guard duties in support of British Army operations in the Middle East. There is a story (I don't vouch for its accuracy) that a British Naval Captain, conning his vessel through the Canal one night, was suddenly surprised to hear the challenge: "Halt! Who goes there?" Swinging his ship's searchlight round, he found that he was being hailed by a diminutive askari standing on the bank, rifle and bayonet levelled at the ship. The Captain, in the best traditions of the Navy, ignored the sentry who promptly loosed off a hail of bullets. The ship was stopped, and forced to remain stationary until an officer from the Regiment could be found to explain to the askari that his duties did not include detaining Her Majesty's Navy.

The Regiment left the Canal Zone with an enhanced reputation for efficiency and skill which it continued to add to during the tedium of the years of peacetime soldiering that were to follow. It was to stand them in good stead when, in 1956, the Battalion was drafted to Malaya as part of the commitment of the then Federation of Rhodesia and Nyasaland.

During this tour of duty, which lasted two years, the Regiment had its first experiences of the techniques involved in fighting against communist terrorists. Today the Rhodesian African Rifles are once more employed against guerillas, and the skills learnt in Asia are again being put to use. But this time the jungles are those of the Zambesi Valley along Rhodesia's northern borders, and the action is not many thousands of miles away but very close to home. Outside the Rhodesian Defence Force very little is known about this continuing operation. It is a bitter little war, hot, uncomfortable and dangerous. Men of the Regiment have already fallen in the fight, and before it is over others will join them. Some are old friends, and if this book has any dedication it is to them, and perhaps particularly to Ken Pierson, that I offer this small, personal tribute.

Bibliography

The *War History of Southern Rhodesia—1939–1945:* J. F. MacDonald.

The Reports of the S.R. Secretary for Defence to the Legislative Assembly—1939–1948: National Archives.

Munchengeti (a series of newsletters from Burma): National Archives.

Newsletters (1944–1946) from Defence Headquarters to the Rhodesian African Rifles in Burma: National Archives.

Huggins of Rhodesia: L. H. Gann and M. Gelfand.

With the R.A.R. in Burma: M. G. Mills (NADA: 26/1949).

Defeat into Victory: Field Marshal Sir William Slim.

The Rhodesia Herald

Account of Operations: April 11–May 8, 1945: Lieutenant Colonel G. Goode.

Roll of Honour

Killed in Action—

Cpl Zwidzayi
L/Cpl Chikangwe
L/Cpl Lazalosi
Pte Kagwira
Pte Sikonzi
Pte Joseni
Pte Ronald
Pte Embruku
Pte Mambwe
Pte Dick
Pte Abero
Pte Takawira
Pte Mundiya
Pte Nyagumbo
Pte Mambo
Pte Chiwoni
Pte Mangoni
Pte Neapiyrara
Pte Shelome
Pte Imonda
Pte Tirivanu
Pte Timotiya
Pte Tawaziwa
Pte Simon
Pte Ndodo
Pte Ruzwidzo
Pte Loya

Died of Wounds—

L/Cpl Crispen
Pte Pikita
Pte Donald

Pte Silombwana
Pte Dimingu

Wounded in Action—

Maj Stirrup, R.
Lt Cummings, H. G.
Lt Sletcher, C. H.
Lt Walker, R. B.
Sgt Chomonorgwa
Sgt Goddard, A. F.
Sgt Mbasela
Cpl Makani
Cpl Mloyi
Cpl Sipanyupanyu
Cpl Samson
L/Cpl Lemesi
L/Cpl Tomo
L/Cpl Macharonga
Cpl Andrea
Cpl Matibila
Cpl Saidi
Pte James
Pte Nyangana
Pte Laison
Pte Vakira
Pte Takawira Jeremiah
Pte Nyikadzanwa
Pte Masweto
Pte Mwanda
Pte Nyamayaro
Pte Msekiwa
Pte Mbondi
Pte Misiri

Pte Hofisi
Pte Levi
Pte Kutshwekaya
Pte Gudzi
Pte Musadadwe
Pte Jonah
Pte Ndaheni
Pte Mateni
Pte Malindi
Pte Henry
Pte Mazinga
Pte Makiwa
Pte Lapken
Pte Jackson
Pte Musiwa
Pte Kamchapela
Pte Misi
Pte Ali
Pte Antonio
Pte Manuel
Pte Paulos Mkalawa
Pte Maskieto
Pte Mtinima
Pte Spiwe
Pte Lameck
Pte Shishawa
Pte Mazwi
Pte Dzingayi
Pte Doba
Pte Diviliasi
Pte Voti
Pte Mutoke
Pte Mdutshwa
Pte Kwangwari
Pte Matshumayeli
Pte Mapanda

Pte Panashe
Pte Nyahuku
Pte Douglas
Pte Koni
Pte James Solomon
Pte Joni
Pte Mubayiwa

Died on Service 1940–1945

WOI Lechanda (R.S.M.)
Sgt Coulthard, M.
Sgt Kenny, G. H. M.
Sgt Egeler, T. H.
Sgt Watson, B. R.
Sgt Daniel, G. F.
Sgt Zilole
Sgt Joel
Cpl Wilson
Cpl Taliya
Cpl Chamba
A/Cpl Yotam
L/Cpl Muyeya
Pte Manyuki
Pte Piyo
Pte Thomas
Pte Dando
Pte Mubayiwa
Pte Chikami
Pte Muzadzi
Pte Kaswurere
Pte Manglazi
Pte Mapurisa
Pte Chigwadi
Pte Fanyana
Pte Hlome

Pte Joseph
Pte Wachekwa
Pte Jack
Pte Kamamanyanga
Pte Mapepa
Pte Chigodo
Pte Malenga
Pte Simasiku
Pte James
Pte Fred
Pte Soda
Pte Musekiwa
Pte Jaisi
Pte Elias

Pte Tawona
Pte Tabanjina
Pte Tagula
Pte Suwake
Pte Ngezi
Pte Semu
Pte Tongwe
Pte Tambudzai
Pte Matake
Pte Kodzayi
Pte Ziwurawa
Pte Johane
Pte Chinyama
Pte Juake